Supporting Children with Autism in Mainstream Schools

Diana Seach

Michele Lloyd

Miranda Preston

The *Questions Publishing Company* Ltd
Birmingham
2003

Continuum International Publishing Group
The Tower Building   80 Maiden Lane, Suite 704
11 York Road   New York, NY 10038
London
SE1 7NX

www.continuumbooks.com

© The Questions Publishing Company Ltd 2003

Text and activity pages in this publication may be photocopied for use by the purchaser or in the purchasing institution only. Otherwise, all rights reserved and no part of this publication may be reproduced or transmitted in any form or by any electronic, mechanical or other means, now known or hereafter invented, including photocopying and recording, or in any information storage or retrieval system, without permission in writing from the publishers.

First published in 2002

ISBN: 1-84190-055-9 (paperback)

Editorial team: Amanda Greenley
                    Linda Evans

Design team: James Davies
                    John Minett

Cover photograph by: Stuart Mills at Sunfield school

With thanks to Professor Barry Carpenter and the pupils at Sunfield in Clent, Stourbridge for their kind permission to use the cover photograph.

Printed in the UK

Contents

1 Introduction
- 1 Features of autism
- 2 Prevalence
- 2 Diagnosis
- 3 The current picture

2 Teaching and learning implications
- 6 Social development
- 8 Emotional development
- 9 Communication development
- 11 Cognitive development
- 13 Motor development
- 14 Behaviour

3 Strategies for supporting pupils in the classroom
18 A child-centred approach
- 18 Language
- 20 Behaviour
- 21 Social skills
- 22 Emotions

23 A whole-school approach
- 23 Assessment
- 26 Classroom organisation
- 27 Accessing the curriculum
- 29 Training
- 30 Liaison with other professionals and parents

4 Case Studies:
- 33 James
- 41 Tan
- 49 David
- 57 Luke
- 63 Louis

- 71 Conclusion
- 72 References

Introduction

The inclusion of children with special needs in mainstream schools remains high on the educational agenda, as evidenced by the Action Programme announced by the DfEE in response to the Green Paper, 'Excellence for All' and the revised Code of Practice (2002). There is perhaps no group of children with special needs who challenge the philosophy more profoundly than those who are on the autistic spectrum. Though all children with autism will share the triad of impairments identified by Wing and Gould (1977), the differences between them preclude the availability of a system or formula that can be applied to their educational provision. What is certain is that people with autism perceive the world in a very different way and that autism is a totally unique way of 'being' rather than a learning difficulty alone.

Features of autism

The triad of impairments include a range of difficulties relating to social interaction, social communication and rigidity in thinking and behaviour. Many of the behaviours which those with autism display are not to be considered as 'autistic' but related to the core difficulties associated with a developmental delay in language, an inability to establish meaning from a range of different social experiences, and reactions to thinking in rigid patterns which help them to make sense of, and interpret, the world around them.

A child may walk through a room full of people, apparently oblivious to them, to pick up a small piece of shiny paper on the carpet. Repetitive 'twiddling' behaviours may be used by children both for distraction from the dominating stimuli and for comfort and security. Similarly there is a predilection towards obsessive interests in certain objects or topics.

Difficulties in all aspects of communication will result in a child having poor use of language, both expressive and receptive. They may echo conversations rather than respond appropriately to them and often interpret language very literally. A little girl with autism was trying on a pair of shoes and was asked by the shop assistant to 'walk up the shop to see how they felt'. She looked confused for a moment and then ran to the other end of the shop and climbed up a ladder that was being used to retrieve shoes on the top shelves.

High functioning people with autism, such as Temple Grandin, have written about the irregularity of how sensory stimuli are perceived by people with this condition. Certain auditory, tactile and visual stimuli may dominate, making it difficult for individuals to 'tune in' at critical times – for example, when a teacher is giving instructions at the beginning of a lesson. Noises like that of a piece of paper being torn may be perceived as loud, threatening or even painful, whereas a sound which would be frightening to most children, such as thunder or an alarm, may be unheard and ignored by those with autism.

Donna Williams (1996) has also described how the features of autism relate to three specific problems:

- problems of control which include compulsion, obsession and anxiety,
- problems of tolerance which include sensory and emotional hypersensitivity, and
- problems of connection which include attention, perception and integration in cognitive processing.

It is these problems which can give rise to a disturbance in behaviour; and children with autism invariably become 'labelled' as having challenging behaviour. An inordinate amount of time can be spent managing this behaviour, yet recognizing the difficulties children are having integrating so much information, and adapting where and how they are taught, can greatly reduce the likelihood of a behaviour outburst.

Prevalence

Autism affects four times more males than females and the estimated prevalence rate for autistic spectrum disorders (asd), which includes those with Asperger syndrome, is approximately 50 per 10,000 people in the United Kingdom (Peacock, Forrest and Mills, 1996). Schools are increasingly recognizing that they may have one or more pupils who fit the diagnostic criteria for the disorder and have planned educational programmes for these children based on individual needs without a formal medical diagnosis.

Diagnosis

Autism can be identified from as young as 18 months, but is frequently confused with other disabilities especially when associated with severe learning difficulties. A diagnosis of ADHD or semantic pragmatic language disorder is frequently referred to in early diagnosis and often deafness is assumed because of the lack of social responsiveness and delay in language development. Children elsewhere on the autistic spectrum, particularly those with Asperger syndrome may merely be branded as 'odd, emotionally deprived or deviant' (Peacock, Forrest and Mills, 1996). Because those with Asperger syndrome are often of average and above average intelligence and have good language skills, a diagnosis may not happen until the child reaches school age. In many instances this may even occur when the child is at secondary school.

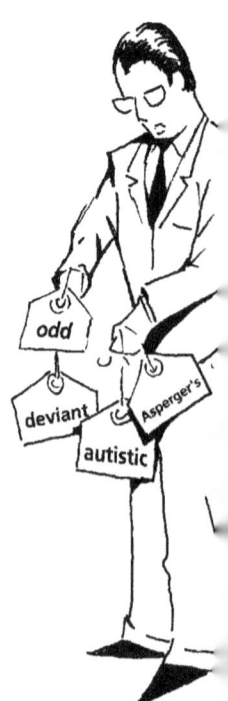

The autistic spectrum of disorders is based on the triad of impairments and classified by the ICD-9 (World Health Organisation, 1978) and the DSM-111-R published by the American Psychiatric Association (1987).

Assessment can often be prolonged and dependent on inter-agency collaboration and referrals amongst different professionals. Teachers, educational psychologists, speech and language therapists, parents and medical professionals will all contribute to detailed assessments based on the child's developmental history and current levels of functioning. Professionals may be reluctant to 'label' a child as autistic whilst parents are keen to have an explanation of their child's difficulties. A diagnosis of an autistic spectrum disorder is invariably the means by which appropriate interventions, educational placement and resources can be established to support a child.

Jordan and Powell (1997) advocate an educational diagnosis of autism and warn against the possible confusion of a medical diagnosis with a diagnosis for education. Regardless of whether or not a formal diagnosis of asd has been made, children who display the characteristics of the triad of impairments need to have a very specialized and carefully tailored approach to their learning needs. This is often difficult to implement in mainstream schools, and local education authorities (LEA's) may advocate different types of provision, in special schools or specialist units in addition to mainstream primary and secondary schools, which may be more appropriate for the individual needs of children on the autistic spectrum.

The current picture

In looking at children with autism in mainstream schools, several interesting issues arise. The first of these is that social integration and relationships with staff and peers are much more problematic for these children than the actual learning that takes place in the formal classroom setting. These problems are of course compounded in the teenage years when relationships with peers and the opposite sex play an increasingly important role in the lives of young people. Social difficulties aside, there are some useful guidelines for teaching children with autism and establishing an environment that is conducive to maximizing the potential of these children in mainstream schools.

Initial reactions to the social environment may give rise to disturbed or confused behaviour which can make it difficult for the child to integrate with their peer group. This is one reason why schools need to carefully consider how the learning environment can be adapted to accommodate these children. Individual or smaller teaching areas can support individual learning needs or provide opportunities for small groups to learn together. In acknowledging that all children, and not just those with special needs, have different learning styles, such considerations go some way to providing a more effective learning environment.

The current emphasis on subject-based learning can be seen as a stumbling block for many children with special needs who require a much broader based curriculum that is significantly child-focused. Rather than regard this as an additional workload for teachers, it is clear that it requires two important considerations. Firstly, that resources are well planned to include the additional support which children with special needs require, and secondly that teachers have the flexibility to develop innovative and creative ways to give children with special needs better access to the curriculum. Jordan and Powell (1997) state that, 'the aim must be not to fit pupils into the National Curriculum but to see what aspects of the latter can be used to meet their needs'.

In our current educational climate, learning is seen as synonymous with academic achievement which can be detrimental to the experience of learning for many children. Children can achieve in many aspects, and it will be important that the various assessments undertaken acknowledge this. For children with autism the need to focus on personal and daily living skills may override the importance of subjects like history or religious education but it is nonetheless their entitlement. Often it is the prerequisite skills such as attending, sequencing and problem solving that are more of a priority for the child. Educational targets set for the child have to reflect the skills a child needs to develop both in personal and academic ways. As far as is possible children should have a significant involvement in the planning of these targets so that they can recognize their own achievements. Prior to the revised Code of Practice document, it was more likely that children were not informed of the targets that had been set and therefore had no means of assessing their own progress. Perhaps the most overriding factor with regards to the inclusion of pupils with autism into mainstream schools is how each school decides on the way in which children can most effectively be educated, and how it reflects the diversity of pupils' needs within the school and the wider community. Policy decisions will have to take into account the nature of the school, how learning is managed and the resources required to maintain good practice, the views of staff in relation to teaching children with special needs, the training requirements for staff and the expectations of all parents.

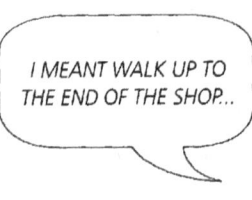

Teaching and learning implications

The nature of the developmental delay in autism has profound effects on how children with autism learn. It also means that each individual will respond differently to learning, and the school will need to consider how to support an individual's needs most effectively. Schools and classes for children with autism will have devised particular approaches for teaching which correspond to the specific impairments of the autistic disorder. However, this may not be as easy to achieve in classes where there is only one child with autism or in classes that cater for children with a range of different disabilities. Initial concerns about teaching a child with autism within the mainstream classroom may be overcome by preparing in the following ways:

- Having an understanding of the specific features of the autistic disorder.

- Recognising the child's individual strengths and weaknesses.

- Acknowledging that the child may have a different developmental profile to that of their peers.

The 'triad of impairments' will affect all aspects of thinking and behaviour, and for a child with autism there are likely to be further difficulties because they will be learning in a social context.

Strategies to support children will be provided in the next chapter, but here it will be useful to look at how the specific areas of development are affected, how this impinges on learning, and how teachers can begin to work with a child who has significant difficulties in socialisation, communication, thinking and behaviour.

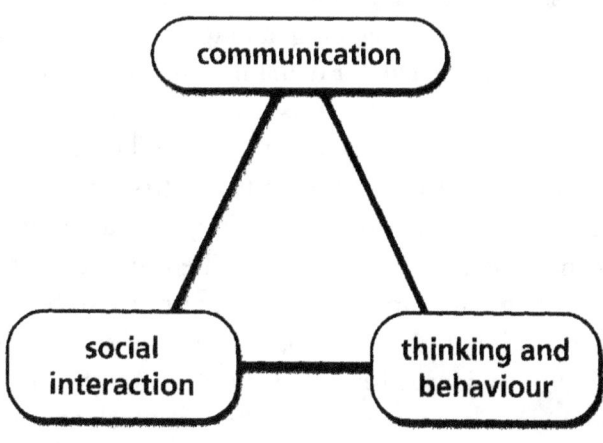

Social development

For a person with autism, much of their social skills training has to be taught as it is clear that not all social behaviours are intuitive. Social relationships require communication at many different levels and if these 'messages' are misunderstood then there will be difficulties in relating ideas and interpreting different social situations. In early development, children often behave by doing something which will gain attention and then there is a flow of interaction which follows. Children with autism have great difficulty with shared attention tasks which involve understanding what another person may be thinking. This is a skill which is vital in any teaching situation and highlights one of the main areas of learning difficulty in people with autism.

Similarly, play in children with autism shows significant developmental delay. From early infancy this occurs when they find an object more fascinating and more predictable than a person. Play then becomes very repetitive or stereotypic. There is a distinct lack of imitative play behaviour and symbolic and imaginative play emerges much later in development. Children who are severely affected may not move beyond the investigative handling or mouthing of a favoured object. Again this has implications for Early Years teaching programmes and some play skills may need to continue to be taught beyond that of the peer group.

Many children with autism do not seek, or even appreciate, social contact but this is not true in all cases. A child may have been taught how to greet a family member or relative but then may use the same strategies when approaching someone they know less well. For most people with autism the teaching of social rules is a life-long process which is further complicated in adulthood by the myriad of rules which apply, or not, to everyone!

The social context of the classroom may pose particular difficulties for a child who has problems interacting with his or her peers and this in turn may affect how others in the class relate to the child. There may also be a lack of desire to interact with others and this can manifest itself in the child engaging in inappropriate social behaviour as a means of avoidance. Donna Williams, who has written about what it is like to be a person with autism in a socially complex world, describes one of the difficulties she has in relating to others as a problem of 'control'. In an attempt to control what is happening around them, a person with autism may use a whole variety of compulsive behaviours and obsessions. The range of obsessions and compulsive behaviours can be extensive, and not necessarily follow any logical or rational explanation, but they do serve an important function for the person with autism, even though they can often overwhelm them. They may be using them to block out the demands of social interaction, an unpleasant experience or anxiety, or because they get a lot of pleasure from either touching, looking at or talking about their fascination. What this means is that the child with autism is likely to use a range of behaviours either to avoid social situations or because they lack the skills to know how to behave.

A lack of social knowledge can also mean that the child either does not or cannot make friends and so lacks the means of being part of a group. Such groups also teach skills like cooperation and turn-taking. The consequence of this is that the person with autism has a weakened sense of the 'self' which can lead to other emotional problems and further feelings of isolation.

If a child has difficulty reading facial expressions or 'body language' they are likely to ignore or even withdraw from attempts at social interaction. This is not the child being ill-mannered. More able children with autism can be taught certain social cues which they can then put into practice when they recognise a particular situation.

Some children also hold great store by learning certain rules and like to point out when others aren't following them. This can be a source of frustration for the adult working with the child, since it is not part of human nature to always behave in consistent ways!

> **Summary:**
> - The child may isolate himself/herself.
> - The child may behave in inappropriate ways.
> - The child may be too anxious to please.
> - The child may have difficulty making friends.

Emotional development

Closely linked to social development is emotional development. Children who have difficulties with effective contact with significant people in their lives will be unable to perceive the emotional states of others. Studies (Attwood et al. 1988; Macdonald and Rutter et al. 1989) have shown that children with autism exhibit significantly fewer facial expressions and less body language than others with mental disabilities. Consequently there can be difficulties in defining a whole range of different emotions.

This is one reason why those with autism will often laugh or cry at inappropriate moments or not particularly show any remorse when told they are doing something wrong. Similarly, parents and carers may make attempts to engage their child in activities which they enjoy only to be rewarded by little expression of pleasure. They may react to particular situations such as the death of a relative, or an accident with little reference to the emotional reactions of others. This should not, however, be misinterpreted as the child being 'unaffected' by such circumstances. They may not express themselves as others might do or necessarily at the time that the incident occurs, but may at some later stage express themselves through their behaviour. Whilst some of the usual emotions may be very evident, such as happiness, sadness, anger and fear, it is often the more subtle ones which those with autism find difficult to interpret or use. These would include being embarrassed, showing pride, being teased, being confident or showing jealousy. Children may come to learn how to react in certain situations but they may still have difficulties understanding why they or others feel the way they do.

Learning about others' emotional states also means that a person can develop a sense of self through their understanding of others. Again, for those with autism this self-concept can be significantly impaired. It is through others that we gain a sense of ourselves, and people's responses to us help us to develop our self-esteem and a sense of self-worth. Children with autism will require considerable support by those who live and work with them to enable them to develop a positive view of 'self'. This is after all one of the ways in which to build personality.

It is through others that we gain a sense of ourselves, and people's responses to us help us to develop our self-esteem and sense of self-worth

---

Summary:
- The child may not understand the feelings of others.
- The child may give inappropriate emotional responses.
- The child will have difficulty interpreting their own and other's emotions.
- The child will have an impaired view of the 'self'.

> Because many children do not understand what communication is for, they may repeat what is said to them, a condition called echolalia

Communication development

The range of communication and language skills found in those with autism is synonymous with the whole spectrum of the disorder. Some children appear to have very good vocabulary but their communication and social use of language remains poor.

The majority of children are likely to have an impaired use of language and difficulties in many aspects of social communication. Once again communication arises from a desire to interact with another person, but if this is absent then, for the child with autism, the intention to relate information will not be as relevant. Similarly, expressing one's needs to another person requires that they be communicated in order to elicit a response, and people with autism will not necessarily have the tools to initiate this. From very early development a young child will learn the basic skills involved in communication regardless of language ability. However, for children with autism it can be that they acquire language but lack the communicative intent to use it effectively. This has significant implications for teaching and learning and will require specific teaching approaches to help children with autism to overcome some of their communication difficulties. Many children are taught language to use in specific contexts and then they have difficulties generalising those skills to other situations or when talking to someone they have not met before. This rote learning of language can mean that the child has a very non-expressive way of talking or they may talk in very pedantic ways, sounding over polite or very formal, even to close members of the family.

Because many children do not understand what communication is for, they may repeat what is said to them, a condition called echolalia, but then not be able to respond to what they have been asked to do. In this instance, the child will need to be physically prompted to the activity so that they learn the meaning of the request.

In addition to the difficulties that children have in communicative intent, it is their lack of skill in how to communicate which is a fundamental feature of autism. It is frequently acknowledged that those with autism have difficulties with the use of eye contact and the social proximity and timing in conversations. These are part of the social rules of communication and to a greater or lesser extent can be taught. Problems in giving eye contact are certainly not evident in all children with autism. Some children use eye contact to gaze at another person to gain attention whilst others may use it only when making requests but not when engaged in other conversations. In the two-way flow of conversation there needs to be an understanding not of what is being communicated but why it is being communicated. People with autism frequently have difficulties in these areas which is why they often appear to stand too close to the person who is talking to them, use odd gestures, or do not appear to be listening when they are being spoken to.

In teaching children with autism there needs to be a greater awareness of the use of language, since continuous narratives, complicated explanations and implied comments will not help the child to attend either to what is being said to them or what they are being asked to do. They have a very literal understanding of language and therefore may not always comprehend the implied meanings, or recognise a joke.

In non-verbal children with autism and in others with language difficulties, the use of symbols or pictures has helped to teach the child to make requests by indicating a particular symbol in the presence of another person. Symbols and pictures can also replace the written or spoken word in showing the child what is going to happen. This can help to reduce any confusion or uncertainty due to a lack of verbal comprehension. Often disruptive behaviours can occur because the child cannot express their needs verbally or because they are unable to make sense of what they are being asked to do when only the spoken word is used. In this instance, behaviours also have a communicative function.

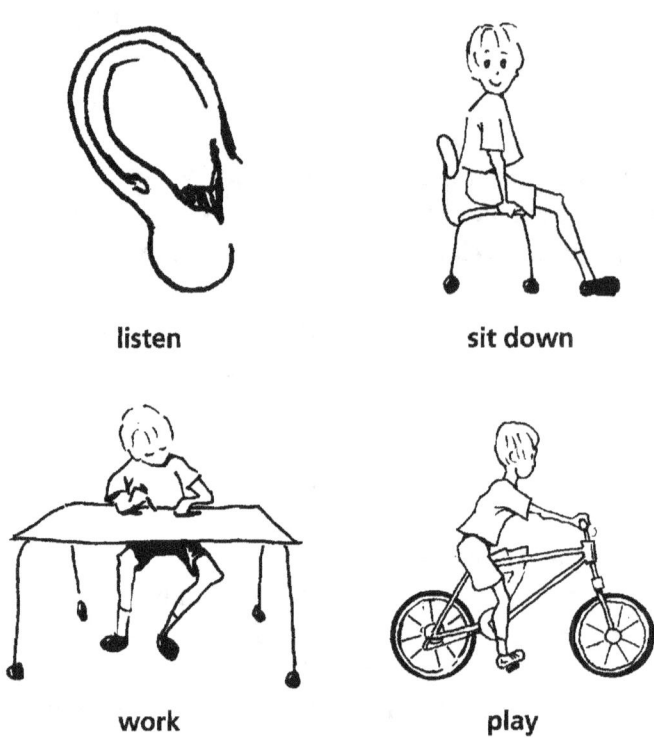

Summary:
- Some children will have good use of language but a poor understanding of communication.
- Children will need to be taught what communication is.
- Children will have difficulties in their use of gesture, facial expression, use of voice, proximity and timing of conversations and will need to be taught the social rules for communication.
- Children have a very literal understanding of language.
- Non-verbal children may use behaviour as a way of communicating.

Problem solving can be an enormous hurdle, especially where this takes place in a social context

Cognitive development

Cognitive ability does not only relate to intellectual functioning but involves thinking, problem solving, memory and motivation. Thinking and learning occurs because of the interrelationship of the cognitive, social and emotional aspects of development. In autism there is a breakdown in this relationship which has resulted in the specific difficulties which those with autism experience (Jordan and Powell, 1996).

Psychologists are largely of the view that an impaired view of 'self' will also result in a lack of awareness of thinking about others and there will therefore be difficulties in problem solving or in seeking out strategies to overcome certain situations. This is one reason why children with autism develop very ritualistic ways of dealing with particular problems. For example, having the same routine for getting dressed every morning or eating the same food, becomes a strategy for knowing how that event will take place. This ritualistic approach to events can dominate all aspects of life for a person with autism and will require very specific approaches to teach a different strategy, particularly where it may impinge on their ability to function in more socially appropriate ways.

Similarly, memory can be very context specific. A child may have an excellent memory for recalling dates on cue, knowing train timetables or remembering routes, but have considerable difficulties with recalling information when they need to work through a particular task. This short-term memory deficit is a particular feature of autism, and strategies will need to be put in place to help the child in these situations.

In a similar way, problem solving can be an enormous hurdle, especially where this takes place in a social context, which the classroom is. Teachers should not assume, for example, that because other children know where the pencils are kept that the child with autism will also know or realise that they can get one without having to ask. Everyday situations can regularly confound the child with autism unless these are identified and the child is given strategies to overcome them, whereas rote learning of dates and numbers will not be such a problem.

Children with autism do find it difficult to make decisions and choices and therefore may not be as motivated as other children in the learning situation to seek out approval for what they have done. Indeed, they may not even see that they have achieved anything but merely completed the task that they were set. Motivation implies that once the learner recognises achievement in a particular task they will be motivated to learn something else. This is not necessarily the case for those with autism. 'Knowing what they know' is often all they feel is important to get them from one end of the day to the other!

Summary:
- The social, cognitive and emotional deficits affect all aspects of thinking and learning.
- The child may have difficulties generalising skills from one situation to another.
- They have good rote memory.
- They have difficulties making decisions and choices.
- They are not always motivated to learn.

Motor development

It is a feature of the autistic disorder that many children will have difficulties with motor development because of underlying physiological problems.

Often a child will develop an odd gait or posture or may be 'clumsy'. Many children walk on their tiptoes and this is considered to have a neurological base. Some children will have low muscle tone and will be reluctant to use their hands to perform simple everyday tasks such as dressing or holding on to objects. This can be related to poor body image and awareness of their own body in space. More able children are often reluctant to take part in physical games or PE because they are aware of their limitations in these areas. There are a group of children who, in addition to a diagnosis of autism, will also have Attention Deficit Hyperactive Disorder (ADHD), and they are likely to have very uncontrolled and erratic movements. Consequently there may be problems of motor control, and children will benefit from physical and movement programmes to help overcome some of these difficulties. Other brain integration programmes, such as 'Brain Gym' or educational kinesiology which encourages the use of the left and right brain hemispheres, have been found to help children to focus and attend to tasks.

Summary:
- Children can experience difficulties with motor control.
- They may have a tendency to clumsiness.
- They may have a poor body image.
- They will require physical programmes to help overcome some of their motor difficulties.

Behaviour

Problems in behaviour can occur as a result of any or all of the features described in the preceding sections. Behaviour difficulties should therefore be seen as a secondary feature of the disorder and not, as is frequently assumed, the 'problem of autism'.

It is inevitable that the rigidity of thinking and behaviour in those with autism will interfere with their ability to learn in a social setting. Some behaviours can be very extreme and therefore disruptive, whilst others may be quite specific to certain contexts and only arise occasionally. Even some obsessional behaviours can be tolerated if managed appropriately by the pupil and the staff. For example, a child may be particularly obsessed with using a pencil with a sharp point on it, and so to prevent them disrupting the class or losing concentration on their work because they are constantly having to get up and sharpen it, they could have more than one pencil available to them when they are working. This could also be a motor control problem. If the child is pressing too hard when writing they could be taught to use less pressure. Often the severity of a particular behaviour is dependent on the interpretation of it by the adults around them.

There will be as many different types of behaviour displayed as there are factors which cause the behaviour in the first place. It will therefore require very careful assessment and management if the behaviour is to be eliminated or reduced.

It is likely that the triggers for the behaviour will fall into certain categories:

- environmental,
- biological, and
- those relating to the rigidity and processing of information.

Many people with autism find that they experience a sensory 'overload' in certain social environments and they can be disturbed by noise, light and even smell. Running away from an unpleasant experience may be regarded as a natural reaction, but in a school context this can be a problem. Classrooms can be particularly demanding places to be when a child is having difficulties understanding the language, focusing on tasks and coping with the social expectations within it. It is not always the case that a child is manipulating the situation by using disruptive behaviour as a way of being removed from the environment, but for some with limited language and social understanding, it may be the

Many people with autism find that the experience a sensor 'overload' in certain social environments and they can be disturbed by noise, light and even smel

Playgrounds can be frightening or confusing places for a child with autism

only means at their disposal. Environmental factors can also include things like the materials and resources a child has to use, the layout of the classroom and the adults working in it. All these will need to be carefully considered if there are attempts being made to understand and manage a particular behaviour.

Epilepsy can occur in association with autism; therefore behaviour is likely to be significantly affected and will require a different approach if the child is to function effectively within a classroom. Hyperactivity is also prevalent in many children, and whilst it may be controlled with medication or diet, it will also require different management strategies. Aggressive attacks on others or self-injury can also be related to a physical problem, such as poor digestion, a headache or even toothache, because the child has difficulty describing such things to someone. Aggression, severe tantrums and self-injury are more likely to occur in children who have significant difficulties with language and communication.

The rigidity in thinking which permeates most daily tasks for a person with autism can result in problems of adaptation to new environments or situations that are not part of a regular pattern. A child may be quite manageable in the classroom setting but display a very different set of behaviours when they go on an outing. Similarly, some resources in the classroom may upset a child and they may then want to only play with one particular toy or activity. A lack of creativity and spontaneity with play and learning about different sensory experiences can often result in difficult behaviours being displayed.

Problems with communication can lead to many situations where the child uses behaviour as a way of expressing a need or an emotion. Playgrounds can be frightening or confusing places for a child with autism and they may display more disturbed behaviours in this situation than in the more structured classroom setting. They may be frustrated at not being able let someone know what they want, feel confused about what they are being asked to do, or not be able to understand why they can't do something that they want to do. An assessment of these behaviours will highlight what the causes are and, from this, management strategies and alternative methods of communication can be implemented for the child.

Summary:
- Problem behaviours are a secondary feature of autism.
- Problem behaviours may be context specific.
- The causes of behaviour may be due to environmental, biological or cognitive factors.
- Problem behaviours frequently occur as a result of poor communication skills.
- Disruptive behaviours will significantly affect the child's ability to learn in a social setting.

Strategies for supporting pupils in the classroom

'Our job as educators of persons with autism is fundamentally to see the world through their eyes and to use this perspective to teach them to function in our culture as independently as possible. While we cannot cure the underlying cognitive deficits of autism, by understanding them we can design educational programmes that are effective in meeting the challenge of this unique developmental disability.'

Mesibov (1988).

It may initially appear that educating a child who has such profound social and communication difficulties within a mainstream classroom will mean that considerable adaptations and expectations will be required by teachers. Whilst it is important that teachers will need to recognise the fundamental differences in the language and learning styles of children with autism, most teachers today are already dealing with pupils in their class who have a range of special needs. It is probably easier therefore to consider that many of the strategies which benefit the teaching of those with autism can also be applied to those with other learning difficulties. Children with autism vary so much in the way that they respond to their learning environment, and this means that teachers will need to be flexible in their approach to teaching them. No two children with autism will ever behave in the same way, but what is similar are their underlying core deficits, the 'triad of impairments'. It is these impairments which teachers will recognise as requiring particular strategies to enable the children to access the curriculum.

Teaching children with special needs does require a much more child-centred approach, and it is here that teachers are often concerned about balancing the needs of the individual and the expectations of government legislation on the education of children generally.

This chapter aims to provide strategies for overcoming some of these difficulties, so that learning and teaching becomes a more positive experience for both the pupil and the teacher.

A child-centred approach

Language

Language is the tool by which all children will access learning. Therefore it is vital for those working with children with autism not only to have an understanding of the language difficulties which these children have, but to consider how language is used in the classroom. However, since language cannot be taught as something separate to the curriculum, it means that there will need to be ways of adapting and using language which makes the curriculum more accessible.

- Provide simple, clear instructions at a level which the child understands.

Some children with poor language skills benefit from a picture or symbol system which enables them to recognise activities and tasks through visual representation. In a similar way, even if a child has good language they may benefit from a supplementary use of symbols or pictures to help them organise and sequence tasks.

- Use symbols or pictures to help the child to initiate communication and understand tasks.

What is of greatest importance is that the child has an effective means with which to communicate, since language is of little use if the core skills for developing and encouraging communication are not in place. Again this is unlikely to occur in isolation but through daily activities which motivate and encourage the child to learn.

Most children with autism not only need to develop an appropriate use of language but also, through everyday experiences, need to learn to use and understand some basic communication skills such as eye contact, facial expression, gesture, social proximity, and timing and content of conversations.

- Provide opportunities to teach what communication is, through everyday experiences and play.

Many children with autism can be very effective readers despite having poor language skills. This can be recognised as a strength, particularly if they have difficulties understanding verbal instructions or are unable to describe a piece of work they are going to do. The child may be able to read to another child who is less skilled at reading, which provides opportunities for supportive learning with their peers. If a child is shy when standing in front of the class to talk about something, then equally they may be more proficient and comfortable if they can read it instead.

- Children who have good reading ability should be encouraged to use this as an alternative method for understanding verbal instructions and planning their work.

Since those with autism have a very literal understanding of language, adults will need to be particularly aware of how they speak to the child. Either the child may not have understood the comment or they may reply in a way which could be interpreted as rude or insolent. This is another reason why they may have difficulties when interacting with their peers, because either they have not picked up the innuendo or have interpreted it in a way which results in them being made fun of.

- Information should be given in context to aid understanding.

Behaviour

Any assessment of a particular behaviour should attempt to identify its underlying cause. Unacceptable behaviour is often a reflection of poor social understanding, difficulties with communication, and the rigid ways in which children think and respond. This may also be in addition to any other learning difficulties, or physical ailments, they have. It is vital to make a careful assessment before any strategy for managing behaviour is put into place.

- What is the behaviour?
- When/where does it occur?
- How long does it last?
- How do staff intervene?
- What is the outcome of the behaviour for the child?

This simple approach will provide evidence for staff and parents about the nature of the behaviour being displayed and how it can then be dealt with.

Staff may then want to consider the following factors:

- Does the child understand the task?
- Is the child distracted by noise?
- Is the child anxious about being part of a large group?
- Does the child dislike certain activities?
- Do the child's obsessional interests and rituals get in the way of him/her being able to attend to work?

Anxiety and stress may be the greatest cause of children's disruptive behaviour and adaptations to the classroom, teaching materials and approaches by staff can go a long way to reducing this:

- Provide a separate table where the child can work quietly and independently.
- Ensure that the child has opportunities to work in both small and large groups.
- Provide written or pictorial instructions so that the child knows what to do.
- Provide short manageable tasks.
- Allow for short breaks between tasks.
- Plan for the child to have a short period of involvement with an activity followed by something they enjoy doing.

Social skills

Since we recognise that the individual with autism cannot be isolated in their learning, it is important that schools provide an environment in which the child's sense of aloneness and confusion is considerably reduced. Interactions with their peers who are of a comparable ability, and not necessarily disability, should provide opportunities for effective social skills training. This can be planned as part of the curriculum and included within the non-statutory framework for Personal, Social and Health Education (PSHE). The significant social difficulties experienced by those with autism can present schools with challenges for inclusion, but this also highlights the responsibility which schools have to take account of the different cultural and social needs of the children they teach.

- Create a classroom environment which has clear social and individual areas and includes a quiet area.

One of the most significant problems for children with autism is a difficulty in making friends or understanding what a friend is for. Some may not even be interested in making friends, but at the same time show a level of tolerance for working and talking with others when they are comfortable doing so. Children can be particularly isolated in the playground or when it comes to partner work in PE or drama. Because those with autism do not always understand social rules, behaviours and expectations, they can find themselves in situations where they can be bullied by their peers. As with any child, such situations should be brought to the attention of those in authority, but the child with autism may not have the ability to do this themselves. Social expectations can be very confusing and they may not even realise that bullying is not an appropriate type of social interaction. If teachers are aware of these stressful times, other pupils can be encouraged to take on the role of a 'buddy' which the child with autism may find less of a threat.

- Use a 'buddy' system to support the child at particular times.

Further work in PSHE can also include Circle Time which is used in many schools to encourage personal and social development. The understanding of all pupils that there is a level of tolerance in social interaction and an expectation for certain behaviours, provides a valuable framework for learning and benefits all the pupils. Other curriculum subjects such as drama, music and movement can emphasise the value of developing supportive and trusting relationships. Often it is these aspects which the child with autism needs to experience, not just the mechanics of how to talk to someone, take turns and how to stand next to them! The aim of any learning experience is that it should be a positive one and this should extend to all pupils, not just those in the class with special needs.

Emotions

Social skills teaching will inevitably include understanding and using emotions. The immature emotional reactions of those with autism will become more evident as they get older, and will therefore need to be addressed more specifically in terms of age-appropriate behaviour.

- Use photographs and videos of children to talk about different emotions.

Developing a concept of the 'self' is also an important aspect of emotional development. One of the ways of discovering a greater personal awareness is through developing more independent skills. The TEACCH approach emphasises this as one of its teaching strategies. The pupil is taught to work independently and, through a system of visual supports and appropriate tasks, learns to function more independently. Adult support is given to teach new skills but, once mastered, the child needs regular opportunities to practise these on their own. This can also be transferred to daily living skills and in this way, into all aspects of their lives.

- Encouraging independence enhances the concept of 'self'.

If a child has difficulty expressing an emotion then he can be given strategies or cues to help him. In a Circle Time session a child could talk about what makes them sad, happy or angry and they could then make a book or poster about it. This will help to establish what elicits a particular emotion, but may also help the teacher to recognise particular triggers for those emotions. Such an exercise may also help the child to recognise the similarities and differences in the emotional states of others. As the child gets older they will need to be aware that they will have to learn strategies themselves to cope with particular situations. Ros Blackburn, a young woman with autism, has the ability to talk in front of large groups of people about what it is like for someone with her disability, but acknowledges that she can do this because of the obsessional objects she likes to hold, which calm her while she is talking. Adolescents will need to be given time to talk through particular concerns they are having, particularly with sexuality and friendship, concerns over their future and so on.

- Develop resources which enable pupils to explain how they are feeling.

- Talk to the child about what they are experiencing so that they can learn to recognise it on other occasions.

The whole-school approach

Developing a child-centred approach does not mean doing something separate or different from the curriculum. Broadly speaking, the 'curriculum' should be seen as the whole ethos, values and organisation of the school and not just something which is taught in discrete subjects. Having an inclusive policy in our schools enables access which acknowledges the unique needs, skills and abilities of all children. Achieving this in the classroom requires teachers to have considerable energy and insight into finding ways of adapting a range of different teaching strategies to meet those needs.

Assessment

The National Curriculum document (DfEE) sets out three principles aimed at giving every pupil opportunities to 'experience success in learning and to achieve as high a standard as possible' (p. 30). Teachers are expected to:

- set suitable learning challenges,

- respond to pupils' diverse learning needs, and

- overcome potential barriers to learning and assessment for individuals and groups of pupils.

Prior to any child with a special need coming into a classroom there will have been several assessments produced, possibly from many professionals and from the parents. These initial assessments will give a good picture of the child's disability and weaknesses in learning. The challenge for teachers at this stage is to try and identify what the child can do, not what he or she can't do, and that the things the child needs to learn are effective and meaningful. The range of assessments for teachers is now vast, and schools or SENCos may have developed their own methods of assessment. In terms of teaching children with autism, it may be more relevant to use something which is autism–specific and therefore gives a clearer picture.

The factors listed on page 24 might be considered.

1. Personal factors

- The ability of the child – their strengths and weaknesses.
- The developmental level of the child and any emerging skills.
- Communication skills, e.g. expressive and receptive language use.
- Independence skills.
- Personality.
- Interests.

2. Social factors

- How does the child relate to peers and adults?
- Do they prefer to be alone?
- How do they behave in a group?
- How do they respond to the learning environment?
- Are they easily distracted?

3. Behaviour

- What type of behaviours are displayed?
- Are there any aggressive or self–injurious behaviours?
- When and where do the behaviours occur?
- What is the nature of obsessional interests?
- What is their reaction to intervention?

The emphasis on recognising levels of attainment at the end of the Key Stages has created difficulties for pupils with special needs, the majority of whom will not necessarily be working on levels within their Key Stage. Whilst the SATs provide an academic score, the child with a Statement of Special Needs will have an Individual Education Plan (IEP) which regularly monitors progress at much shorter intervals. Individual targets highlight specific areas of need and usually highlight skills required to access a particular subject of learning. The P level descriptors for English, mathematics and personal and social development, which are used to support the target-setting process, mean that the child's skills can be identified, and there are then opportunities to set further targets so that progress is recognised. In addition, a child presenting with behaviour problems will have an Individual Behaviour Plan. All these should be seen as useful tools for assessment, contributing to a whole picture of a child's strengths, and helping to inform practice and curriculum content.

Classroom organisation

Considering the reorganisation of a learning environment for a particular pupil or group of pupils might be thought of as over-emphasising the specific difficulties a child may have. On the contrary, it offers a level of support to a child and provides them with better access to learning. Pupils are unlikely to be in a situation where they have a permanent learning support assistant (LSA), and therefore the classroom should enable the child to access appropriate materials and tasks when the assistant is not there. It is not a good idea for a pupil to have too much support otherwise the child becomes dependent on their assistant and can develop a sense that they don't need to learn to be more independent. The teacher will also need to know that the child can be as responsive to them as they are to the learning support assistant.

In terms of classroom layout, pupils will prefer an individual work area but will also need to experience working in a group. The child will learn when different activities require them to be part of a group and when they can work independently or with support where they sit. Materials should be accessible and labelled so that they can access these independently.

It is impossible to begin to analyse the extent of the social interactions which are expected within the learning environment, interactions that some people take for granted but which children with autism can find very daunting. It may not be, as might be assumed, that they don't want to work, but that they do not have the confidence or skills to ask for the things they need in order to get on with the work. Similarly, pupils in secondary schools should learn to use a timetable and carry it around with them, this helps them to locate where they need to be and what they are going to do. Primary classrooms, however don't always have a timetable on display which the child can refer to. For children with autism this can be vital, and knowing what they are going to do will help pupils with their organisational skills, and also their behaviour. Finding and using resources which, as best as they can, help to reduce anxiety and frustration can be the key to the child feeling able to cope in a very demanding social environment.

- Use a classroom layout which helps to support the child's access to learning.
- Use visual information which encourages the child to be more independent.
- Use resources which help reduce anxiety and frustration.

Accessing the curriculum

The National Curriculum provides a framework for learning for all pupils, and there is now a greater emphasis on the inclusion of pupils with special needs.

Given the patchy acquisition of skills which characterises children on the autistic spectrum, it would be inappropriate to suggest that they do not benefit from a subject-based curriculum. All children typically show preferences and aptitudes in different subjects and will excel at those which motivate them. This pattern of learning is no different for a child with autism. Some of the core skills such as using language, attention, turn taking, organisation and social skills will not necessarily be taught in isolation from the curriculum, and the subject areas provide opportunities for both shared and individual learning experiences. It is recognised that children with autism relate well to a more structured approach to learning and the different subjects provide just that. They provide the child with some idea of what will be taught in that lesson, whether it will be a class, group or individual activity, where it will be and, for secondary age pupils, who it will be taught by.

The National Literacy and Numeracy Strategies also have clear guidelines for how lessons are structured and use tasks that show progression in the acquisition of skills. The task for teachers is not to see children with autism as being unable to access subjects like the majority of pupils in the class, but to consider how those tasks can be differentiated to support positive learning outcomes for all pupils. It is not about adapting *what* is taught but differentiating *how* it is taught. Not all children, for example, find it easy to sit on the floor or concentrate for a specific length of time. What are the expectations? Children are more likely to attend if the time slots are shorter, individual difficulties can be addressed and skills reinforced in one-to-one sessions, particularly those which relate to their IEP targets.

A definition of differentiation may be hard to come by, but most teachers and certainly inspectors will recognise it when they see it. So before looking at specific subjects, how can work be differentiated to meet the needs of children with autism?

- Tasks should be shorter.
- Time slots for work sessions can be shorter.
- The language used should be understandable to the child.
- Tasks should be supported by visual or written instructions.
- Computer-assisted learning is of particular benefit.
- Individual one-to-one support should be provided.
- Functional, practical activities to explain work should be used.
- The child should be enabled to make links with other subjects, e.g. cross-curricular activities.

In English, pupils may have particular difficulties with writing, may need more time to produce a piece of work, and may require additional resources such as a pencil grip or access to a computer. A great emphasis has been made throughout on the importance of language. Instructions will need to be carefully directed at the pupil and questions made clear and unambiguous.

Many children with autism excel at mathematics because they enjoy the rote learning and answers follow clear, logical patterns. As far as possible, practical activities should be used to help the child consolidate their understanding.

Similarly, science provides opportunities for the exploration and interpretation of natural phenomena. Many children with autism have obsessional interests in this area, from a very sensory level to a desire for more detailed explanations of the forces of nature. Practical activities can also aid understanding.

Geography and history may hold similar fascinations for details and dates. Map reading is a recognised strength and the long-term memory skills of children with autism enable them to have a good awareness of the features of places and buildings.

If a child has a motor control problem and finds PE difficult, they may require additional support from a physiotherapist or occupational therapist who can provide alternative activities, but these can still be part of a movement curriculum.

Art, music, drama and movement/dance can enable a more creative expression of skills and can be used to support other areas of the curriculum. Again, pupils may excel in these areas and should be given support to be able to do this, such as learning a musical instrument, joining an art club or going swimming.

What this section highlights is that while recognising that the routes to learning may be very different for pupils with autism, they have access to the same cultural, spiritual and social experiences as their peers. It also gives them opportunities to develop levels of independence and advocacy in accordance with their potential. Some children may need considerably more support in this but it is nonetheless their entitlement.

Training

A vital aspect of school development is to identify the training needs of its staff in relation to the nature of pupils it aims to support and teach. It has become increasingly recognised that most schools will be working with a child on the autistic spectrum, and knowledge and understanding of the disorder is vital if the school is to take a positive move to include these pupils. Local education authorities have a responsibility to provide such training needs, but these will only occur in response to schools identifying such needs. It is somewhat ironic that to teach a child with a sensory impairment, teachers are required to have a relevant qualification and yet it is not the case for teaching children with other disabilities.

Training will be important, not just for the teacher receiving the child into their class, but for all staff to develop an awareness, since they will inevitably come into contact with the child at some stage. Not only is this important in terms of understanding the child, but it also helps to provide support for the staff member who has the child in their class, who may just need opportunities to express any concerns or behaviour management strategies with a colleague.

Training is often assumed to be relevant only when it is seen as something separate from the general everyday running of the school. However, training and staff development should be seen as an extension of what is happening in the classroom, with schools making regular opportunities for staff discussions and support as well as INSET. Most schools now have a teacher as a SENCo and it will be their role to liaise with staff with regard to their training needs. Quite importantly, this should also include training for learning support assistants, who will have a very special role in working specifically with a child. For many teachers, developing specialist knowledge of a particular aspect of special needs comes from an individual interest in that area, and this is why many teachers will take on distance learning courses or higher degrees in order to extend their own professional expertise.

- Identify training needs for teachers and learning support assistants.
- Knowledge and understanding of the disorder informs teaching approaches.
- Staff should be supported in wanting to developing their professional expertise.

Liaison with other professionals and parents

Legislation has highlighted the importance of close liaison with other professionals (Revised Code of Practice, DfEE, 2002) when working with children with special educational needs. These are most likely to include those working in the health and social services but may include voluntary organisations as well. Statutory assessments will inevitably involve many professionals and these, with parental wishes and expectations, are taken into account when deciding on an appropriate placement for a child. All of these contributions will also have a significant effect on any progress or educational achievements the child will attain in subsequent years. It is therefore vital that schools can work in close liaison with other professionals, and develop effective partnership with parents so that they can be regularly informed of their child's progress and learning needs. After all, parents have a very specific knowledge and understanding of their child, which can go a long way towards enabling both the school and the child to ensure that learning is an effective and positive experience.

- Other professionals will be included in statutory assessments.
- Partnership with parents promotes effective outcomes.

The final section of this book describes five case studies of children, aged from nine to fourteen, who have been successfully included in mainstream settings.

Through careful observations in schools and patient discussion with pupils, staff and parents, the authors are able to illustrate in some detail, the component parts of effective good practice. Readers are given a unique insight into the difficulties experienced by pupils with autism and how these manifest themselves in everyday classroom life.

Case studies

James
A Year 9 pupil with an informal diagnosis of Asperger syndrome.

Tan
A Year 8 pupil with high-functioning autism.

David
A Year 3 pupil diagnosed with autism a year ago.

Luke
A Year 7 pupil with Asperger syndrome.

Louis
A Year 8 pupil with Asperger syndrome.

James

James is a Year 9 pupil who attends a large urban comprehensive school. He comes from a large family and some family members share his social and communication difficulties. Although the family live in very close proximity to the school, his mother feels that James and his brother, William, are inappropriately placed and she has tried to have them educated elsewhere, at both special schools and neighbouring comprehensives. Special school places were denied to them as they were both assessed as being of at least average intelligence. James is being supported in Key Stage 3 and William is statemented for a social and communication disorder.

Diagnosis

James has had no formal diagnosis of an asd, but informally he has been diagnosed by teachers as having Asperger syndrome. Despite the informal rather than formal nature of his diagnosis, the specialist teacher at the school is of the opinion that James receives the same amount of support that he would if he had been statemented. Characteristics associated with Asperger syndrome are evidenced in James's communication skills. He is very precise in his speech and has a pedantic way of describing things. He also speaks in a flat, monotonous tone, yet with great fluency at times and using a sophisticated range of vocabulary. He seldom engages in eye contact with people he is communicating with unless prompted by others to do so.

Social interaction

The main area of difficulty for James is social interaction. His communication skills tend to exacerbate the difficulties he has interacting socially. According to the specialist teacher, "His language is often pedantic, which is not good for his street cred". James is also prone to tangential behaviour manifested as inappropriate laughter which is sudden and obsessive. The laughter is often about a cult television series. He is easily irritated by his peers whom he perceives disrupt his classes and prevent him from learning. Until recently he would enter a classroom and tell other pupils to be quiet. The main priorities for James at the moment are learning the skills of surviving peacefully among his peers, one approach being to learn to ignore his irritation at their behaviour, and learning strategies to manage his own behaviour, for example laughing inappropriately. The learning support that James receives consists of one lesson a week with the specialist teacher which is one-to-one and lasts 50 minutes. In mainstream lessons, but not all, a learning support assistant is present to help James as well as other students in the class who require support.

There is a whole-school policy for facilitating the inclusion of pupils on the autistic spectrum. The school's SENCo is pushing to raise awareness of asd and there is a growing consciousness of asd within the school generally. The specialist teacher emphasised that: "It's a very moral, very organised, very just school. Every single member of the school has equal rights... There's a whole team, supporting these students the best we can".

Additionally, the county autistic society plays a key role in heightening the profile of autism and this seems be to filtering into mainstream schooling. In-service training at the school has, and continues to be, targeted at learning about asd, especially in the last two years. Although in-service training is available to teachers and learning support assistants alike, it is currently conducted separately. Staff believe it would be beneficial to have some in-service training together so they could learn from each other. The school has around 50 statemented/SEN students and their relatively large number appears to contribute to their acceptance in school.

> The main priorities for James at the moment are learning the skills of surviving peacefully among his peers

Mainstream lessons

James does not require academic differentiation: his problems are social. He is capable of accessing the whole curriculum and, with additional support at Key Stage 3, he follows National Curriculum programmes of study in all subjects. To gain insight into his experiences of mainstream schooling, James was observed in some mainstream lessons. The learning support assistant was not present in the lessons observed. The first lesson was a drama class which was relatively unstructured and involved group work. James stood stiffly near the stage and did not communicate with anyone else for the duration of the lesson and appeared withdrawn. In the meantime, the teacher and other pupils worked around him. In a later conversation with James he revealed that he had not known what to do in the lesson because his usual working partner had been absent.

A different picture emerged during a geography lesson attended by James in which the teacher taught at the front of the class. James was likewise sitting at the front and appeared fully engaged. He listened with interest and made occasional notes. The tight structure of the lesson seemed to provide an environment in which James was comfortable and consequently better able to learn.

Classroom strategies for enhancing the learning of some pupils with Asperger syndrome include minimising distractors (Connor, 1999, p. 85; Barnes, 1996, p. 10). This was borne out during an observation of a German lesson. At the suggestion of the German teacher, James habitually sat at the front of the class as he tended to lose concentration otherwise. In this way the German teacher was better able to maintain his attention. Additionally, James could see the board more easily as his table was directly in front of it.

On the occasion of the observation of the German lesson, pupils entered the class chatting and sat in groups. James, on the other hand, entered alone and sat in his usual position at the front by himself, adjacent to the teacher's desk. At times during the lesson he had difficulty concentrating when the class became noisy. However, the teacher maintained James's attention periodically throughout the lesson by standing near him and keeping him on task. This seemed to be easily achieved due to their close proximity. At one stage the teacher wrote example sentences on the board which pupils were to write in their exercise books. The teacher asked James four times, individually by his table, if he understood the task. It was clearly beneficial that his table was near to where she was standing. The teacher asked other pupils about their work but not as often as she did with James. While other pupils chatted as they worked, James completed the task in his exercise book in silence. The teacher was very encouraging to all the pupils and gave them all a commendation for their work, including James. At the end of the lesson the pupils exited in groups, chatting, while James left by himself. He did not speak socially to any peers throughout the lesson. Work-wise, though, James seemed to manage well in the lesson. Like the geography lesson described above, the German lesson was a structured teaching situation with clear instructions from the teacher to all the students as to what to do at the various stages of the lesson. Despite the absence of any social engagement with peers, academically James seemed to benefit from teaching strategies such as being set achievable tasks and being encouraged with prompts and reminders to complete his work (Barnes, 1996, p. 12). Being at the front of the class enabled him to work relatively un-distracted by others and facilitated regular communication with the teacher.

One-to-one lesson with the specialist teacher

James had been having a one-to-one lesson each week with the specialist teacher at the school for more than a year and they had developed a good rapport with one another over this time. In addition to providing a secure environment for James, these lessons provided a forum for social as well as curriculum-based discussion. Within such lessons James and the teacher sat at right angles to one another, as depicted here:

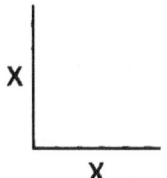 This formation gives space to the pupils writing hand, promotes eye-contact and allows for shared attention while simultaneously diminishing overcrowding.

During an observation of one of these lessons the teacher began by asking James general questions about how he was feeling and about his family and home life. It was immediately apparent how very chatty and forthcoming James was, a notable contrast with some mainstream lessons observed previously. Amongst other themes he chatted about 'killer' whales and about what they eat, such as seals. He expressed strong disapproval of the name 'killer' whale since it portrayed them in an unfavourable light. He was evidently very knowledgeable about nature and said it was a subject he was interested in.

The teacher let James know the structure of the lesson, informing him of what they were going to talk about. When she asked James if there was any school work he wanted to discuss they talked about his science assignment and the teacher gave him some advice about it. As he retrieved the assignment from his bag, it emerged that he had bits of paper in his bag that he no longer needed. The teacher put a bin next to James for him to discard paper. Children with autism can benefit from a stable, ordered environment, though they may require help in achieving and sustaining this. In matters of a more straightforward nature, James appeared organised without external intervention, as exemplified in his large, unfolding pencil case in which his many pens were arranged in the colour of the rainbow.

The teacher had James's IEP to hand which she referred to and wrote on during the lesson. After finishing talking about the science assignment the teacher returned to more informal chatting. James revealed how he had to wait to use the computer at home while his brother used it. Yet James felt that he was patient, volunteering the comment, "Patience is one of my strong points". The teacher asked if that was because she had taught him to be patient, and he agreed. The teacher reminded him that he had not always been patient, and that he used to tell others in class to be quiet which they did not like. James remembered and agreed.

The teacher gave James a commendation for the day's lesson. He showed her a certificate he had been awarded for getting 20 commendations. Again, he volunteered this and seemed immensely proud of the certificate. When the teacher suggested that he could put it on his bedroom wall he thought he probably would. Mindful of his dislike of PE, the teacher reminded him not to forget his PE kit in future.

Towards the conclusion of the lesson James spoke about photographs his mother had of him and his siblings, taken when they were younger. He then referred to his earliest "unaided memory" (his term). It was when he was six years old, and he was running away from someone in the playground because they were being horrible to him. He was keen to talk about his first unaided memory which evidently made a considerable impression on him. Evident too was that the setting's comfortable atmosphere facilitated such expression from James. During the course of the lesson he talked about a wide range of topics, illustrative of his tendency to wander from subject to subject. He clearly enjoyed talking to the specialist teacher, as though he was afforded little opportunity generally for talking and for someone to listen to him. Such inclinations were also identified by the specialist teacher at interview, whose views are explored further in the next section.

The view of the specialist teacher

The specialist teacher underlined the importance of developing James's social interaction and communication skills. Consistency was the key behaviour strategy she was using with James, which entailed working to a known method at a known time. James is resistant to change, and consistency was thought to be a way of enhancing his sense of security. Another strategy used by the teacher was making James explain himself, and asking him what he meant, in order to aid his communication skills and self-confidence. His communication skills were further addressed through speech and language input with the specialist teacher, which was sometimes task specific and other times general language input. Included in general language input is the teaching of metaphors to illustrate how words can be ascribed meaning beyond their literal definition. The specialist teacher identified which activities elicited the most positive responses from James: "Allowing him to talk, even allowing him to be tangential. He does obviously enjoy it. We try and make time for that if there's no more pressing demand. I consider it to be a vital part, for him to be able to express his view points in his particular way". She rewards James with much praise and commendations as well as listening to him: "It's a reward for him to be listened to. He likes to be listened to".

Targets, behaviour strategies and rewards are written into James's IEP. James was involved in setting his own performance criteria since IEPs at the school are written in conjunction with pupils, with their understanding and full cooperation, and are signed by pupils. The setting-up of James's IEP was informed by observations of the specialist teacher, the school SENCo and the concerns of other teachers, and is reviewed in this light once a term. Liaison between professionals is of crucial importance in effecting a whole-school approach to supporting pupils with autism. To this end, pupils' IEPs are circulated to house co-ordinators and then, at need, to individual teachers. Where particular issues emerge, IEPs will be referred to the SENCo and other learning support staff. The specialist teacher liaises regularly with James's tutor, house coordinator and the SENCo. Parents too are informed about the content and development of their child's IEP.

The system of rewards and sanctions used in the school is deemed applicable and effective for James. He is proud of his commendations which the specialist teacher discerns are beneficial in raising his self-esteem. His relationships with teachers are good and he carries out tasks very well. On the subject of inclusion in school activities, the specialist teacher noted that James is the class representative voted in by other pupils. At first teachers had wondered whether James was being set up by his peers. Yet their suspicions appeared to be unfounded when James proved to be an effective representative: because he is so pedantic he ensures issues are raised and followed through.

An area in which James continues to have difficulty, however, is social situations. He does not function effectively in a group, swaying between being 'street cred' and withdrawing. According to the specialist teacher, he tends to focus on the teacher in classroom situations and will volunteer comments. She explained that James's conduct made it difficult for him to make friends: "He is still different. He claims to have some friends but his behaviour often militates against this. He makes demands of friends".

Although James experiences difficulties functioning in a group, the teacher commented that he is able to work independently and in some situations might prefer to do so. Another area he needs help in is active, objective reflecting and taking into account other factors in events that occur. An obstacle to such reflection, though, is James's inclination to withdraw. In view of his social interaction difficulties, the specialist teacher emphasises to James that characteristics relating to social interaction are learnt – people are not born with these abilities. To illustrate her point she explains to James that she has taught him the importance of being patient and that patience is a characteristic that people learn. James himself recognises that he has learnt to be more patient, as revealed during the one-to-one lesson described above. Such self-analysis and recognition are a measure of James's gradual development. While social interaction problems continue, the specialist teacher is of the opinion that James is making progress: "He's not radically changed but he's learning to manage his behaviour".

> *He does not function effectively in a group, swaying between being 'street cred' and withdrawing*

Tan

Tan was diagnosed in his mainstream primary school as having autism. Before he transferred to secondary school, his parents, learning support assistant and headteacher from primary school accompanied him on a one-day visit to an Autism Integration Unit attached to a large mainstream comprehensive school which he now attends. He is a Year 8 student with high-functioning autism. With no general learning problems or adverse behaviours, it is only upon close contact with him that his difficulties become apparent. His main area of difficulty is social and life skills. Intellectually he is very able and is in the top set for maths in which he excels. Yet although he can do complex mental mathematical calculations, he is unable to tie his shoelaces. He is introverted, and staff at the Autism Integration Unit are working on building his self-esteem. Despite being a high achiever, Tan does not recognise success within himself.

Chinese culture

Tan's background is Chinese and he speaks Chinese at home, though he himself was born in Britain. He has some problems understanding the English language and needs additional help in this area. In the past it was assumed that his difficulties were due to his language problems, which could account for why he was not diagnosed with autism as early as he could have been. Tan is very well mannered and polite. He has a great respect for authority and abhors violence. Tan's mother is very keen for him to do well at school. Tan himself acknowledges that he has a lot of homework and that he must complete it all: "I don't want to let my mum down". He is extremely conscientious and often worries about his school work and achievements. One of his older siblings gained a First at Oxbridge which may exacerbate his desire to achieve academically.

The main priorities for Tan at the moment are for staff at the Autism Integration Unit to learn the signs of his anxiety and to develop effective ways of reducing it. They have identified Tan's eczema as a barometer for his level of stress, worsening the more stressed he becomes. It is not always obvious, however, that he is stressed and he needs to be asked at regular intervals whether something is troubling him.

Autism Integration Unit

The integration unit enables students on the autistic spectrum, like Tan, to attend mainstream school and receive additional individual and group support at the unit. Pupils must have an autism-specific statement as part of the entrance criteria to the unit. Eight pupils, all male, currently attend the unit, which will have its maximum capacity of 16 during the next academic year. Indeed, the unit has had to turn away pupils wishing to attend next year because it is fully subscribed. The head of the unit noted that people are getting to know of the unit and that places there are like "gold dust". Next year the unit will have 2.4 teachers. The unit also has learning support assistants who accompany students from the unit to mainstream lessons in which they require additional support. This is on a 1:1 or 2:1 student/staff ratio. LSAs are subject related, in that students have the same LSA for certain subjects. There are LSAs in the main school learning support centre who support mainstream SEN students.

Unit students come to the unit for morning and afternoon registration, morning break and lunchtime. Reverse integration is promoted, enabling the friends of pupils at the unit to visit the unit at break and lunchtime which are open times. If they so wish, pupils from the unit can attend the main school canteen at lunchtime accompanied by an LSA from the unit. Tan currently does so twice a week. Attending the canteen is encouraged by staff.

The unit consists of two main learning rooms, separated by a staffroom and a small quiet room. The quiet room is used for private work with pupils. Every pupil at the unit has their own individual work bay in either one of the two main learning rooms which they always use and where they eat their packed lunches. Work bays are also used for one-to-one lessons with pupils in subjects in which they require additional support. When pupils have a lesson at the unit they commonly mirror the lesson that is taking place in the mainstream class. They generally manage well during lessons at the unit since it is coping with the surroundings in mainstream that poses difficulties, rather than their academic abilities. During one-to-one lessons at the unit when pupils undertake work requiring concentration, the individual work bays help to minimise distractors (cf. Connor, 1999, p. 85). Each work bay consists of a table and upright screen in front of the table, on which most students pin their timetable, some pictures and some rules of the unit.

The rules of the unit include:

- We should be nice to each other at all times.

- If we upset someone we should say sorry.

- We should smile a lot.

- We should use proper manners – putting your hand up
  - speaking in turn
  - looking at who you are talking to
  - being polite.
- We should try to help people.
- We should try to say something nice to each other here every day.

One of the main learning rooms has a computer accessible to pupils during recreation time. The unit has a television and videos which pupils can choose to watch at lunchtime. There is an enclosed garden at the rear of the unit used by pupils, including Tan, during break and lunchtime for football, softball, chase, hide and seek, etc. The unit also has board games to help pupils integrate and interact. The entrance/exit to the unit displays a sign reminding pupils to take their pens, pencils and books to lessons across in mainstream.

Being an integration unit the same reward system is used in the unit as the main school, comprising merits for good behaviour and academic performance. In addition, staff at the unit have devised a system of coloured behaviour charts that are specific to the unit. The charts were introduced in response to a significant number of boys refusing to attend mainstream lessons. The charts involve colouring in a blank timetable for each pupil, with different colours denoting the type of behaviour displayed by a pupil during each lesson. It is a quick method of recording behaviour and a visual image for the boys to see how they have behaved. An individual's chart can be compared from week to week to identify any times of the week that are particularly difficult for the pupil. Staff believe the boys regard the charts as an incentive for good behaviour and also a deterrent against bad behaviour.

None of the pupils at the unit are disapplied from any areas of the curriculum. Special provisions have been made though in relation to PSHE and PE. PSHE has been adapted for the pupils, and is conducted at the unit in two pupil groups rather than in mainstream. Due to the tendency among pupils towards a lack of co-ordination, and their customary need for guidance concerning physical activity, pupils at the unit attend PE lessons together conducted by a teacher from the unit. Additional areas of support provided for pupils at the unit are speech and language therapy, and social and life skills through Circle Time.

Mainstream lessons

Like other pupils at the unit, Tan has LSA support in the majority of his mainstream lessons. According to the lead LSA, Tan manages well by himself in French and history and no longer has LSA support in these subjects in order to aid his inclusion in mainstream. A flavour of his experiences in mainstream was gained through observing him in lessons accompanied by different LSAs as well as in lessons where no LSA was present.

Tan and Nick, another boy from the unit, were to have a mainstream geography lesson accompanied by a unit LSA. It is beneficial for pupils with autism to be prepared for transitions between classes (Jordan and Jones, 1999, p. 54) and to this end the LSA asked Tan what lesson he had next. Tan replied "geography". In the geography lesson, the LSA sat next to Tan to offer him more support. Tan interacted periodically with a girl sitting next to him. The geography teacher asked pupils, including Tan, some questions and he gave the correct answer. The geography teacher then set pupils the task of writing up their fieldwork notes and Tan asked the LSA to clarify the teacher's instructions on the board. The LSA also helped two other pupils sitting nearby when they requested his guidance. At the end of the lesson the geography teacher set some homework which the LSA wrote in Tan's homework diary. The LSA and Tan conversed regularly throughout the lesson. The LSA praised Tan during the lesson and patted him on the back by way of encouragement.

The LSA subsequently attended a technology lesson with Tan in which pupils were constructing battery-operated clocks they had designed. Occasionally, the LSA helped other pupils in the class in addition to Tan. It was a lively lesson with much movement among pupils and Tan was anxious about the likelihood of completing his clock. When working with Tan, the LSA continually asked him work-related questions and explained aspects of work to him. Through adopting this approach he helped and guided Tan rather than carrying out tasks for him. The LSA described Tan's finished clock as 'smashing'. Tan was very conscientious and likewise pleased with the clock which he planned to put in his bedroom.

A similarly boisterous atmosphere emerged during a science lesson attended by Tan accompanied by the lead LSA from the Autism Integration Unit. In the science class Tan and the LSA sat next to one another, though the LSA was mobile for much of the lesson, helping the science teacher with classroom management. Tan appeared to work well with intermittent help from the LSA.

In contrast to the bustling, fluid character of the technology and science lessons, a more structured learning environment was evident in a history lesson attended by Tan independent of LSA support. The history teacher opened the lesson by asking pupils to perform a brainstorm exercise. While other pupils proceeded with the work,

Tan seemed not to understand the task. Without his help being requested, the history teacher directed Tan individually on three occasions before Tan commenced the set task. The teacher later dictated some sentences. When his dictation included a difficult name he pointed to the name in Tan's textbook for Tan to see it, though he did not do this with any other pupils. Pupils were set another task and Tan again failed to embark on the work until given further individual instructions from the teacher. After the lesson the history teacher spoke of his aim to keep Tan on task which was achieved in that day's lesson. With regular contact and additional instruction from the history teacher, Tan was able to accomplish the set tasks.

The view of the LSA

Tan's progress at school and the role of the Autism Integration Unit were discussed at interview with the unit's lead LSA. She emphasised the importance of teamwork among staff at the unit: "I think that the team and the adults responsible must be strong and firm together, working together in whatever practice is decided or whatever style."

Teamwork with mainstream teachers was deemed vital too: "You need to be able to work as a team so that you can gently say, and feel comfortable about saying to the teacher, 'Sorry, but my boy from the unit won't be able to do that, or can't do it, or it will distress him'… You have to talk to the teachers and build up a relationship for the sake of the child".

The LSA engages in team teaching with mainstream teachers, as evidenced during the observation of the science lesson described above. She explained that if a class teacher can set the lesson, there should be opportunities for the class teacher to spend time with the child from the autism unit while the LSA undertakes general support around the class.

When the LSA supports Tan in mainstream lessons she endeavours to enhance his inclusion where possible. In practical lessons, for instance, if pupils are instructed by the class teacher to form groups, Tan will not approach other pupils. The LSA will ask some pupils if they are willing to work with Tan. If they agree, she advises Tan to ask them to work with him. Other pupils seldom ask Tan to work with them without being prompted, because they are aware that there is something different about him. The LSA discerned that mainstream pupils are far more tolerant of pupils from the unit due to the fact they have an LSA with them: "I think that we [LSAs] do actually act as a huge buffer". In line with Connor's (1999, p. 85) recommendation, the LSA provides mainstream pupils with information about autism and the difficulties that someone with autism might experience in a fundamental, basic way. For example, she would explain to them that Tan is very clever – it is just that he may not always understand what they say: "It's quite amazing how well the others would react to that. And they'll say, 'Oh well, that's all right'. I think it is a matter of getting them to understand what the difficulty is because it's not as apparent as other difficulties".

Information about Tan is passed onto other members of staff through a system of record keeping comprised of tick lists such as 'homework completed' and 'he interacted with small group in class'. In addition, LSAs at the autism unit keep a record of a pupil's experiences when they are with them. When Tan's annual review is due, a form is sent to every subject teacher for their evaluation of his progress. The form includes comments on Tan's academic as well as social progress.

It is in the area of social interaction that Tan's difficulties are most apparent. He is unable to engage in academic integration and social integration simultaneously. He has some friends, and one close friend in particular. The LSA perceives that Tan is respected and held in awe by some of the mainstream pupils, though he himself does not recognise this and it does not affect him in any way. A couple of girls have come to the unit on reverse integration at lunchtimes specifically to be with Tan, but he does not regard this as anything special. According to the LSA, Tan does not meet other children out of school. Time away from school includes extra maths tuition. The long-term aim is for Tan to be fully integrated into the main school which the LSA believes is achievable.

On the subject of training and support, staff at the autism unit are regularly circulated with literature and videos from the SEN officer, speech and language therapist and educational psychologist. The unit's lead LSA attended a 10-week course on autism and education without which she believes she could not do her present job. She would welcome more in-service training: "I don't think it does to just go on one course and say that is adequate. It has to be on-going and it has to be built on that foundation because it's so complex." She discerned that support for LSAs was necessary too: and the need for LSAs to have someone they could speak to who understands the pressures of their role.

Circle Time at the Autism Integration Unit

Another aspect of the LSAs' role at the autism unit is conducting Circle Time with pupils to develop their social and life skills. The Circle Time was observed during a lesson conducted by the lead LSA with another LSA also in attendance. Three Year 8 pupils on the autistic spectrum were present. The group's participants sat around a table facing one another and, at the direction of the lead LSA, commenced by greeting each other. The lead LSA presented a toy dog and explained that each time a group member was holding the dog they could say a rule that would apply to the group, such as having hands on the table. Each group member proceeded to devise a rule when in possession of the dog.

The subject of the lesson was learning about appropriate and inappropriate behaviour. The lead LSA cited the example of shouting and asked one of the pupils, Max, whether it was appropriate or inappropriate to shout in an exam and at a football match to which he gave the correct answers. The other pupil, Harry, answered correctly also when she asked him about the appropriateness of running in a race and in a classroom. The lead LSA then asked Max when it was appropriate to laugh and he responded, "When watching comedy programmes". She asked Harry the same question but he could not think of an answer. She reiterated the question to Max instead who said, "At the circus". When she asked Harry what in particular at the circus would make people laugh, he replied, "Lions". Max interjected, saying, "No, people would laugh at clowns". The lead LSA suggested Harry look at Max as Max was helping him, thereby encouraging eye contact between the boys. The lead LSA asked Harry how he could let her know he was listening to her. Harry did not know. The lead LSA asked whether his ears wiggled and Harry replied, "No". She asked him again how he could let her know he was listening to her. Eventually Harry said by looking at her, to which she replied, "Yes".

The focus of the lesson turned to playing hangman. Both pupils had a turn at writing on the board. The lead LSA praised Max for looking at the other group members each time they guessed a letter. At the end of Circle Time, the lead LSA instructed group participants to say goodbye to each other and to say something nice to each other about what they had learnt in the lesson. As before, group members could speak only when holding the toy dog. When Harry said goodbye to the lead LSA, he thanked her for teaching him about appropriate and inappropriate behaviour.

Activities beyond the academic curriculum, such as Circle Time, are evidently of key importance in facilitating the academic as well as social integration of pupils on the autistic spectrum. The lead LSA at the autism unit was optimistic about the philosophy and practice of integration in the future: "I'm absolutely certain that it can work. But integration like this is really quite a new venture."

David

David is nine years old. His parents first noticed he had developmental difficulties when he was 18 months old. He has attended his current mainstream primary school since Reception class and has had one-to-one teaching since then. At the end of Year 1 he was back-classed a year, repeating Year 1. He is now in Year 3, a year behind his age group.

David was diagnosed with autism a year ago. Prior to starting school he was diagnosed as having difficulties of a social and communicative nature. The main reason why he did not have an autism-specific diagnosis earlier was because he was possibly engaging in imaginative play. A difficulty associated with autistic spectrum disorders is limited imagination, particularly sharing in the imaginative thought and play of others (Jordan and Jones, 1999, p. 5). One of the educational psychologists involved in David's diagnosis felt he was engaging in imaginative play. Yet his teachers believed he had learnt responses through having structured activities with his LSA. Rather than spontaneous imaginative play, he was re-enacting activities he had rehearsed exactly word for word. At the time of his diagnosis of autism David was using very little language, almost exclusively one-word utterances. He had no awareness of other people around him, no eye contact and his behaviour was challenging.

According to his mother, David's strengths are having a good memory and being very good at the computer. He was previously obsessed with trains but now has more wide-ranging interests. David's mother described how he likes to have things in order and does not cope well with change. His parents have to repeatedly explain the reasons for any change of routine to allay his anxieties. They are pleased with the progress he is making and believe he is happy and comfortable at school. His mother has regular contact with teachers and they also communicate through David's reading diary.

Social skills

Like his parents, his teachers regard social skills and social integration as one of the main priorities for David at the moment. Additional targets on his IEP include developing understanding and use of spoken language, and developing concentration and listening skills. His IEP was set up by his class teacher, LSA and the school's special educational needs co-ordinator. Targets written into the IEP are relayed to his parents, who are informed of the termly IEP reviews. David does have opportunities for setting his own performance criteria at a very simple level but not for his IEP. He is unable to work independently beyond brief stints and would be unsure how long to work on a set task and unsure when it was complete. At times he does structured activities very quickly. Akin to some others with an autistic spectrum disorder,

David is sensitive to light and noise. He is affected by the weather, preferring bright, sunny conditions, when his mood seems to be more favourable.

Mainstream

A further priority at the moment is making David's transfer to his new mainstream school next year as smooth as possible. He is presently visiting his new adjoining school twice a week with his LSA. He has met his teacher for next year and is borrowing reading books from the school's resource room. One of the LSAs David is to have next year has been coming on outreach from the new school to work with him for five hours a week for half a term. His existing LSA continues to work with him during this period. David formerly had learning support assistance for 15 hours a week, two-and-a-half hours funded by the school and 12-and-a-half by the LEA. Since his last review, the LEA funds four hours of support a day, totalling 20 hours a week.

When planning the curriculum for pupils with autism it is important that its content is child-centred rather than subject-centred in order to address pupils' needs (Jordan, 1996, p. 6). In David's case he is unable to access much of the Year 3 curriculum and accesses subjects at his own level through individual programmes of study for most areas. The class teacher differentiates for three to four ability levels within the class and David's lesson plans are separate, though not necessarily in written form. For instance, in maths he would work on the same form of calculations but with numbers smaller than those used by the rest of the class. He attends Circle Time and PSHE with other pupils and discusses matters further with his LSA where necessary. Handwriting poses great difficulty for David and he is following a handwriting programme advised by an educational therapist. To improve his motor skills he has a tray of practical activities for developing a pincer grip, pinching movements and twisting movements. Tasks such as handwriting practice are undertaken on a one-to-one basis with LSA support in an area staff and pupils refer to as David's 'office'.

David's 'office'

David previously attended all lessons with the rest of his class. However, staff became concerned that he was disrupting other pupils, swinging on his chair, unfocused and refusing to work even with the accompaniment of his LSA. Staff decided to set up an area where David could receive individual input from his LSA with less distraction from the busy class environment. David's 'office' is a screened area positioned at the entrance to the open-plan classroom. Within it he has the resources he needs to work independently for short periods or to work with his LSA. There is a lap-top computer on which his LSA is teaching him to type due to his handwriting difficulties. The LSA uses a hand-

> Staff are not deterred from sticking unhappy faces when necessary, rather than always happy ones, as it is important to show David what is acceptable and unacceptable behaviour

held whiteboard to write work on for David. Other table-top activities, easily available and clearly labelled, include speech and language packs, games, reading books and activity cards used in conjunction with the tape recorder. His LSA has a formal discussion with his class teacher once a week to discuss work with David for the week ahead.

David's weekly timetable is pinned to one of the two upright screens of his office, showing pictorial and written details of each activity throughout the day. A new display is attached to the timetable if a different activity is taking place to alert him to the fact that there is going to be a change to routine. Details on the timetable consist of two colours to distinguish periods with the two current LSAs. A behavioural chart is pinned on the other screen of David's 'office'. When he behaves well, staff attach a sticker with a happy face to the chart and an unhappy one if he misbehaves. On the advice of an educational psychologist, staff are not deterred from sticking unhappy faces when necessary, rather than always happy ones, as it is important to show David what is acceptable and unacceptable behaviour. The chart is completed on a weekly basis, providing David with a visual record of his conduct. If he works very well he receives another type of reward sticker and certificates from the class teacher which are applicable to the rest of the class too.

Although David's 'office' is just outside the classroom, teachers are aware that advice generally recommends maintaining pupils in the classroom where possible. The nature of the school is such that classrooms are open-plan and have curtains which are closed only during quiet teaching periods or during registration. David's 'office' is situated in a shared area used by three open-plan classes. He is not separated by being in that area, yet is afforded his own space.

Classroom observations

Observations of David and his LSA were carried out, offering some insight into his educational experiences. During a morning's registration with the rest of his class, David appeared preoccupied with the move to his new school, asking aloud which teachers he would have there. After answering his questions, his LSA had to ensure David paid attention to the class teacher's instructions. His LSA is using the strategy of social stories with David to enhance his inclusion in whole-class situations. Written by his class teacher and speech and language therapist, the social stories are structured accounts concerning how David should be behaving in different situations with the rest of his class. In addition to being a social integration target, the social story is a listening target. His LSA reads through the social stories with David at regular intervals. An example of a social story is illustrated below, focusing on how David should listen to his class teacher, Ms Day.

Illustration of a social story

Listening to the teacher

When I come into the classroom, the other children sit on the carpet in front of Ms Day's chair.

The children will be sitting upright on their bottoms with their legs crossed, ready to listen to Ms Day.

Ms Day sits down and starts talking.

When Ms Day is talking, the children are trying to listen carefully. They are listening to Ms Day so they know what to do next.

I will try to sit upright on my bottom with my legs crossed and look at Ms Day, listening to what she says.

Listening to Ms Day will help me to know what I have to do next.

Ms Day will be happy if I sit quietly and listen to what she says.

Although David is sometimes reluctant to go to the screened area known as his 'office' and expresses a preference to stay with the class, according to his LSA he does not need much persuasion to work in his 'office'. He was observed working with his LSA in the setting of his 'office'. While the rest of the class embarked on work set by the class teacher, David's activity involved playing with four cloth dolls referred to by staff as the family. Play of this kind aims to stimulate his *imagination and improve his communication abilities*. Straight away he started telling a story about the family of dolls. He was very talkative and imaginative, using his own ideas without prompts. His LSA noted that he would not have engaged in such play a year ago, even with prompts. The manner of David's play was not locked singularly into his own imagination, but he responded to input and questions from both his LSA and his class teacher who visited during the story with the dolls. He enjoyed playing with the dolls and would play with them for longer if allowed.

Regular contact with the class teacher was also maintained when the LSA engaged David in a speech and language exercise in the venue of the screened 'office'. The LSA showed David one of a set of printed pictures from the speech and language therapy service. The LSA asked him questions about the picture to practise drawing inferences, solving problems and assuming different character roles. David's short concentration span became apparent and he had to be kept on task throughout the exercise. His lack of sustained attention was also in evidence during an ensuing handwriting exercise when once more his LSA had to keep him focused on the set task.

Concentration

David's wandering concentration was further revealed when his LSA asked him to check with another LSA, whom he knew, whether they were going to play a game. On leaving his 'office' area he walked to a nearby window before eventually approaching the other LSA, who confirmed they were to play a game. In a communal area shared with other classes, David took part in a game with four children from his class, two of whom had English as their second language. The game entailed children describing characters on hand-held picture cards they had been dealt and other children identifying the characters on a large visible picture board. David's LSA sat next to him and repeatedly asked him to listen to the other children. She continually endeavoured to draw him into the game and remind him of the rules. He was good at describing his characters when instructed, but mistakenly disclosed the identity of one of them by pointing to it on the picture board. While the other children won around 7–10 points each, David did not get any. Yet he did not mind and indeed seemed unaffected by the outcome of the game. His LSA concluded that he was capable of listening on a one-to-one basis with an adult but that listening in a busy group was too much for him. Despite the game serving as a forum for interaction, David did not interact with the other children. He is able to be in a group physically but not engage socially.

A more positive response was forthcoming when David read through a story book with his LSA. He enjoys reading and has good intonation. He is experimenting with language at the moment and is prone to repeating names he seems fascinated with. His LSA encouraged him to think of rhyming words, though on the occasion observed he could not think of any. He also enjoyed returning from his 'office' to the main classroom and being asked by the class teacher to call out each child's name, thereby releasing them to go to lunch. The game showed he knew about 80 per cent of the names and was a way of maintaining his involvement with other children. David's contact with children in social as well as academic terms were themes considered at interview with the school's SENCo, whose views are discussed further in the next section.

The view of the SENCo

The school has a whole-school policy for integration and the SENCo emphasised that David is regarded as part of the class: "All the times when [the children] are sitting on the carpet between sessions he will be with them, perhaps with his support assistant beside to keep him on task or keep him involved in the discussion. Equally there are times when he needs not to be doing what they're doing, and again we endeavour to have those activities running along-side what the class are doing. I think because of the nature of the building partly, but also his particular difficulties, there are times when he needs to have the space to come away from the class and work in an area that's more enclosed. And so it tends to be a general class introduction and then he might go off to a table or he might go off to a space outside the classroom to work and come back together at the end. So he is considered, like any other child, a part of the class but with needs which need to be flexibly met".

The SENCo explained that, when assemblies and special occasions like Christmas or school performances are held, staff need to prepare for these events and ensure that David has extra provision in place to participate. Staff prepare David by practising events with him and spending more time with him before they take place. Rehearsing events entails going to the part of the school where they are to be held, walking around, and informing him of who is going to be present so he knows what to expect.

The benefits of adapting the curriculum for David were described by the SENCo. Previously teachers felt that they were not meeting David's needs and that he was not making progress with writing. Since he has been in Year 3, an educational psychologist has advised teachers to give themselves permission to feel that David does not have to strictly follow all programmes of study. In the words of the SENCo: "It might be equally important for him to be listening to a music tape, using other sensory inputs, rather than trying to access something that is less useful to him in terms of life skills".

Another departure from the formal curriculum is when David is occasionally afforded time away from his own classroom to work with a teacher he has developed a special bond with. As she does not work full time she has the flexibility to work with David and accompany him to the Reception classes where he enjoys helping the younger children. Staff believe these occasions are beneficial to the younger children and David alike.

Because David spends time away from his classroom, the system of sanctions and rewards used in the school is not always applicable for him. Wider school sanctions include removing a student from a classroom. This would not be suitable for David as he would need an immediate explanation of what he had done wrong and advice on remedial action. According to the SENCo, it is important to talk over

> "It might be equally important for him to be listening to a music tape, using other sensory input rather than trying to access something th is less useful to him terms of life skills"

with David what has happened rather than excluding him from the classroom: "There are times when he does need to leave the classroom because he's become agitated. So it would be wrong to give him the message that he's been naughty at those times".

In terms of rewards, mentioned above, David receives stickers and certificates for good work in line with the rest of his class. As an additional reward, specific to him, he is allowed extra time on the computer, which he enjoys, and this reward is written into his IEP.

David is making progress socially. The SENCo detailed some of the strategies employed to enhance his social interaction at school: "He has had a lot of planned programmes where, for example, he would have a book with photographs of all the children that were going to be in his new class over a summer holiday, and something about each child – their name and what they like doing. So we have tried to plan for him becoming aware of other children. He has moved to working alongside them, getting to know children's names in the class, even saying, 'I like him, he's my friend'".

Rather than being non-communicative as before, David will now say 'hello' to other children and respond to their questions. He has also learnt that other people want him to make eye contact.

David has some friends who look out for him in class. One girl in particular takes him under her wing and ensures he knows what he should be doing. He meets friends outside school and plays well with his two brothers, but he does not have any close friends. His LSA previously spent break and lunchtimes with him yet he reacted adversely by running away; it appeared he viewed these occasions as his own time. She now spends recreation time with him two days a week. She steers him to other children and other children to him, but the engineered interaction is short-lived. David prefers to be alone.

On the subject of professional liaison, school staff have regular contact with outside professionals including a physio-educational therapist and a special educational needs officer. Speech and language therapists produce an annual report on David. The SENCo would, however, welcome greater continuity regarding contact with external agencies. She noted that David has seen around four educational psychologists and six speech and language therapists since being at school, resulting in teachers not having the continuity to build on David's previous reports. Outside professionals are nevertheless willing to attend school at the request of teachers. An educational psychologist, invited by the SENCo, recently gave a talk to all the school staff about autistic spectrum disorders to raise general awareness among staff.

Looking ahead to David's long-term development, the SENCo was encouraged by his progress hitherto: "I do think he's benefited from the social integration of being here and sometimes he really amazes me and he suddenly makes a big leap in a certain area. Recently it's been in telling stories with an adult as a scribe. He has suddenly developed this ability to re-tell a story in detail. I would say I've always had grave concerns about his ability to cope in society independently but I can't be sure because he does surprise you with spurts of development".

Similarly, David's mother has aspirations that he will be able to learn to drive, get a job and lead as independent a life as possible. David would like to become a baker and his mother hopes he achieves his potential.

Luke

Luke was observed in his primary school and subsequently went on to a secondary school where his parents feel that he is managing well with the level of support that he is receiving. Luke, now 12 years old, was diagnosed as having Asperger syndrome when he was ten. At three years old he had been referred to a speech and language therapist because of a severe speech delay and language difficulties. He began his full-time education at the local primary school but it soon became evident that he would require greater support because of his speech and language difficulties. The statementing process was initiated and after the second term he transferred to a Special Support Facility(SSF) for children with speech and language disorders situated within a primary school. This school is in a neighbouring town and meant that Luke had to be transported there on a daily basis.

Special Support Facility

There are two classes in the SSF catering for Key Stage 1 and 2 pupils, and Luke attended both of these with the exception of the last two years when he transferred to the mainstream Year 5 and 6 class where he was fully integrated. The SSF supports eight pupils in each class, of whom several are on the autistic spectrum but without any formal diagnosis other than that of speech and language difficulties. Both classes are staffed by a teacher, a learning support assistant and a part-time speech and language therapist. As its name implies, the SSF enables children to attend their mainstream class for registration and most curriculum subjects. English and mathematics are taught in the SSF where there is a greater emphasis on the teaching of language skills and literacy. Science is also taught in the SSF but with opportunities for reverse integration where pupils from the mainstream classes come into the SSF. In these classes there are a number of children who have a Statement of special educational needs for other learning difficulties, and it is felt that they benefit from some of the approaches and teaching strategies used in the SSF classes.

Mainstream

The level of support offered to individual children extends into the mainstream classrooms and this enabled Luke to transfer to the Year 5 and 6 class. Since a large number of children who come into the SSF have a diagnosis of an autistic spectrum disorder, the school is generally well informed of the difficulties that children with this disorder experience. His teacher had known Luke for two years and, although he had not been involved in his initial assessments, had worked with another child with Asperger syndrome, which he felt had given him a good understanding of Luke's difficulties. The current method of writing IEPs in the school did not allow for children to set their own performance criteria and Luke's IEP had been prepared by the teacher from the SSF who is also the SENCo. He was supported by a learning support assistant whom he saw for seven-and-a-half hours a week. Luke's class teacher felt that the main priorities for Luke were his time management skills and his responses to following advice. Luke could work independently but did not produce a lot of work. His learning support assistant was helping to keep him on task in lessons and also gave him specific sessions on literacy. During the observation of Luke in an English lesson when his learning support assistant was not present, he spent very little time on the task which the teacher had explained to the whole class. He was not distracted by other pupils talking around him, nor by the computer on the table next to him, which had a moving screensaver. However, he spent a lot of time rocking on his chair. One of his IEP targets was to focus on his motivation and organisational skills. This particularly related to his imminent secondary transfer, so Luke was spending time in the SSF to prepare for going to secondary school. All IEPs are reviewed termly and the class teacher felt that the parents were happy with the targets the school had set. As Luke had been in the school a number of years, the school felt that Luke's parents had always been very positive about his needs and achievements.

Behaviour

Luke's general behaviour was considered to be manageable. He had on occasions had outbursts when he had not understood what was expected of him, and had hit out at others when he did lose control. He tended to be by himself in the playground but often attracted attention to himself by making 'silly' noises and flapping his arms. He also did this in assembly. His teacher found that talking to Luke in the aftermath of an incident helped to calm him down and he was able to discuss alternatives to his behaviour which Luke appeared to take on board. The school has a reward system for good work and behaviour and, in addition to this, the SSF uses tokens for listening and talking which are added to marks on the merit system used in the rest of the school.

Curriculum

Luke was in a class of 25 pupils and took part in all curriculum subjects with the class. Occasionally he was withdrawn from assembly to work in the SSF with his assistant. Setting for all the pupils was only done for mathematics and Luke was observed in one of these lessons. He knew where to find the equipment he needed but didn't have the correct book to work from so had to share. He got on with the work set, albeit at a very slow pace, and he didn't always follow the teacher's strategies. Luke was able to tell me on another occasion that he liked geography, history and science because he liked learning facts and of course enjoyed using the computer. He found English and

> *He tended to be by himself in the playground but often attracted attention to himself by making 'silly' noises and flapping his arms*

mathematics quite hard and didn't like PE and music. He has motor control problems and disliked running. Consequently, he tried to avoid doing PE because he didn't want to be laughed at by other pupils.

Social interaction

Luke appeared to be accepted by his peer group in the class but there was little evidence of any social interaction other than with his brother. His brother also has speech and language difficulties and attends the SSF. As there is only a year in age between them they were often taught in the same class group. A Circle of Friends had been tried with Luke to encourage him to be more interactive in the playground but he appeared not to be bothered either way whether he had friends or not. On the occasions when Luke was observed he seemed to be on the periphery of what was happening in the class. He was not forthcoming with offering information even when the teacher spoke directly to him. If his attempts to answer the teacher's questions were not acknowledged then he appeared disgruntled and lost track of what he was supposed to be doing.

Learning support assistant

When Luke had his learning support assistant with him, there was a greater awareness of where he sat in class so that he was more in the centre of what was happening. She also found that she could motivate him to work by suggesting he used the computer or looked in other books for information he needed. She also used egg timers and a time check system to keep him on the task. Some of the methods that the teacher had used to encourage Luke to work he had also found useful for other children in the class, for example, the PSHE curriculum which included Circle Time, had been of benefit to several of the pupils.

Positive ethos

Within the school there is a positive ethos of supporting and integrating children with a range of different learning difficulties. Regular staff meetings keep staff informed of individual children and where children are moving from their mainstream class to the SSF, there is a liaison between the teachers to ensure that the child's curriculum needs are being met.

Luke's parents felt that the school had contributed to the progress that both their sons had made. They were realistic about what they felt was important for Luke and his brother but were anxious that such levels of support would result in them finding it difficult to cope independently when they moved to a secondary school. For this reason, Luke's parents had carefully considered a secondary school for him which would continue to give appropriate levels of support whilst recognising that he needed to learn how to manage more by himself.

Secondary school

The secondary school they chose for Luke is relatively small and its special needs department was already working with other children who have Asperger syndrome and high-functioning autism. He is now receiving two hours a week teaching time in the special needs department for help with his English and social skills. He is supported in his other subjects for 12-and-a-half hours a week but this is not on an individual basis. The learning support assistant remains in the class to help children when required. Luke says that he likes this because then the attention is not just on him. It is early days for Luke in his new school but his parents report that he seems to be enjoying it. Like any young person, he is not always forthcoming about what he has done at school and his parents are having to accept that he won't initiate telling them about it. However, his parents have regular correspondence with the teacher in charge of the special needs department.

Luke continues to have difficulties organising his PE kit and getting changed on time. He is coping with finding his way around the school to get to different lessons, but this is because he is currently being 'shadowed' by the learning support assistant. Luke's parents spend time trying to explain to him that now he is older he has to do more for himself. They are providing him with a lot of support to help him do his homework and to organise this around his free time. Luke would like to be more independent, but his parents are concerned that he would find it difficult if it involved asking other people to help him. He is particularly keen to go on a train by himself and so his parents are trying to plan for him to go on a short trip with a familiar person at either end of the journey.

Luke's mother describes his difficulties in this way: "He is normal up to a point when he finds thing difficult". They have to choose the right time to ask him questions as he doesn't like to be confronted. He keeps to routines and if questioning interferes with these then he doesn't like it. Although he is not keen on PE at school his parents thought that they would try him at a Karate Club and he now has his second Brown Belt. Again, he likes the routine of what happens in the session, but his mother still feels that he does what is asked of him because he is there and not necessarily because he wants to be.

His parents' biggest concern is over his safety, now that he is getting older. He is quite wary of older children, which is why he prefers to be by himself in the playground. Also he has a very precise, pedantic way of communicating with others as well as a very literal understanding which his parents feel may get him into trouble. Similarly, they are also concerned about sex education for Luke. His parents say that he has been taught things at school which he doesn't appear to fully understand and that they can only then explain what he asks them at a level he can understand for himself. Although it is some years away, his parents are already thinking about what life will be like for Luke when he finishes school. They hope that by then he will have developed an interest or skill in a particular area that he could use for employment. As his mother says, "Let's hope he can get a job in computers, then he'll be happy!"

During one of the observations when Luke was in the class with his brother, they had been allowed to move around the classroom to find a dictionary. Steven, his brother, had been set a different activity from Luke and as he walked past him he said, "This is hard isn't it, Luke?", to which Luke replied, "Life is hard, Steven".

Louis

Louis, a Year 8 pupil, was diagnosed with Asperger syndrome while in his mainstream primary school and now attends a mainstream secondary school. His mother died from an illness when he was seven. Louis, an only child, and his father subsequently emigrated to an English-speaking country. However, in addition to being bullied at school, Louis did not receive much needed in-class support resulting in their returning to England after three months.

Obsessional behaviours

Like most, if not all, children with autism, Louis developed obsessional behaviours (Jordan and Jones, 1999, p. 38). When he first came to secondary school he was preoccupied with moving his hands, twirling them around and shooting with them. This has transferred to playing with his hair and shoelaces, which was distracting for other pupils in class. Teachers recently suggested to his father that he acquire a stress ball for Louis to play with so as to be less of a distraction to others.

Educationally Louis is making progress, but socially he experiences a number of difficulties. He does not understand the boundaries of social interaction nor what behaviour is appropriate and will, for example, poke people to get their attention. As a result he often alienates his peers with his unsocial behaviour. Although teachers at the school have informed other pupils of Louis's problems, they recognise it is difficult for pupils to understand why Louis behaves as he does.

Mainstream

Louis is not disapplied from any areas of the mainstream curriculum, though he dislikes PE and makes excuses not to participate. His speech and vocabulary are very good and he writes and spells well. He is in lower sets across subjects areas, although the French teacher is keen for him to move to one of the higher French sets next year as he is very able in this subject. Occasionally, Louis receives special worksheets from different subject teachers, produced in conjunction with the SEN department, that are easier for him to complete. Such worksheets are employed with some restraint by teachers however, as Louis's abilities need to be continually stretched: otherwise, teachers fear, he will simply take the easy option. Apart from French, in which he undertook the standard examination paper, Louis sat the SEN papers in other subjects and achieved favourable marks.

Learning support assistant

Louis receives individual support from an LSA who attends most mainstream lessons with him. He is entitled to 20 hours of support per week from the LSA, which is paid for by the LEA and out of the school's budget.

As well as accompanying Louis to mainstream lessons, the LSA attends morning registration with him. However, the LSA believes it is beneficial for Louis to attend registration by himself some days in order to develop his independence.

In addition to in-class support, some pupils with autism will require support in less formal arenas, as was the case with Louis. At his primary school he would invariably be waiting at the school door ready to come back in after break or lunch. When he first came to secondary school he was likewise first back to lessons after break times. This period was referred to by his LSA as 'the bad times' when Louis was bullied. His LSA subsequently joined him in the playground or remained indoors with him in order to help him with his homework. He was reluctant to venture outside by himself with other pupils. The close relationship between pupil and LSA can unwittingly result in the LSA becoming the pupil's only friend (Jordan and Jones, 1999, p. 53). Perhaps Louis sensed this, because for the last two months he has resumed going outside during break and lunch, unaccompanied by his LSA. Interestingly, this was his own idea and is an indication that he is gradually becoming more sociable. He seems to get on well with other pupils, joining in with them and playing football, and coming back into school at the same time as them. Occasionally he will spend break or lunchtime with his LSA if he has homework for which he wishes to enlist her help.

> Louis managed to block out the disruption of others and proceed with the work in hand

Curriculum

Since Louis does not receive full-time support, his LSA needs to be flexible and she consequently attends classes where support is deemed to be most needed. Less support is required in English and French, for example, so the LSA does not attend all lessons in these subjects. Louis was observed in mainstream lessons both with and without the accompaniment of his LSA. In lessons where the LSA was in attendance she and Louis always sat together. During observations of a maths lesson and music lesson, Louis worked well, volunteering answers to questions posed by the class teachers. Louis and his LSA engaged in work-related conversation on a one-to-one basis as the need arose during the lessons. Though the LSA was the person with whom he interacted predominantly, there was some interaction between Louis and the class teachers and, to a lesser extent, with his peers.

Louis and the LSA worked through word exercises together set by the English teacher for the whole class. He managed to block out the disruption of others and proceed with the work in hand. He did not interact with peers during this lesson. Not all students with Asperger syndrome would behave likewise and many are indeed susceptible to distractions. Louis's sustained concentration was probably facilitated by the presence of the LSA.

During the English lesson there was no interaction between Louis and his peers and minimal interaction with the English teacher. It was with his LSA whom Louis interacted primarily. This resonates with Jordan and Jones's (1999, p. 53) observation that the role of the LSA may evolve to the extent that they are invariably the person who supports the child with autism. Other lesson participants, namely the class teacher and other pupils, may be unintentionally excluded. Other lessons attended by Louis gave rise to different interaction dynamics. The degree to which a pupil with an ASD interacts with others in the classroom will be influenced by variables including the personality of the class teacher, the behaviour of other pupils, the content and atmosphere of the lesson, the presence of a LSA, and, not least, the pupil's own personality.

Louis's level of classroom interaction during a RE lesson contrasted with that of the English lesson. The RE lesson was led by a teacher with a rigid style of teaching who began by selecting children to read aloud passages of a story in the Bible. He then asked pupils questions about the story. Louis responded by putting up his hand numerous times, as did others, and was chosen by the teacher to answer some of the questions. When answering one of the questions, Louis continued talking and the teacher, although praising him, had to halt his protracted monologue. Pupils were set the tasks of copying out the story and answering questions about it in their exercise books. Since Louis is very precise but slow when writing, the LSA started copying out the story for him in order that he kept pace with the other children. Louis subsequently assumed the task of writing himself. It was a very structured, controlled lesson with clear instructions for work written on the board by the teacher. Louis remained engaged throughout the lesson, evidenced in him repeatedly putting up his hand to answer questions.

It is beneficial for members of staff to liaise with one another on the progress of the child with autism, and after the RE lesson the class teacher and LSA engaged in such discussion. They agreed that Louis sometimes did not know when to stop talking, as had been apparent during his elongated answer to one of the RE teacher's questions. In addition, the LSA applauded the RE teacher for maintaining Louis's attention and for having eye contact with him. The LSA is encouraging teachers to engage in eye contact with Louis, and for Louis to likewise look at teachers during communication – an area in which he is improving.

Louis is able to work independently for a limited period and when the learning environment is conducive. During an English lesson for quiet reading, for example, when his LSA was not in attendance, Louis read happily through his book by himself. He enjoys reading and was the quietest pupil in class, chatting briefly with his neighbour.

The view of the learning support assistant

The nature and level of support required by Louis in school were themes explored in an interview with his LSA. She noted his tendency to interrupt teachers in class by putting up his hand and waving at them which she has to instruct him not to do. Another of Louis's tendencies is to talk at the same time as the class teacher, and to then elicit information from other pupils in class that he has missed from the teacher. The LSA is discouraging him from doing this as it is distracting for other pupils.

Louis has further difficulties staying focused and on task, and tends not to follow teachers' instructions properly. According to the LSA, if Louis is required to read a text and answer questions about it, he will start answering the questions first and consequently miss the point of what he is doing. The LSA has to ensure Louis works his way through the various set tasks. She explained that her role also involves reassuring him about his work: "My role basically is getting him through the classroom situation, getting the work down and stopping him panicking because as soon as a teacher says something, he thinks he can't do it.

In a similar vein, Louis has made excuses not to do his homework because he thinks he is unable to do it and panics. To help him overcome his anxieties, his LSA writes down his homework for the weekend in a homework diary. SEN staff informed his father who monitors the homework and signs the diary.

The main targets that staff are working on in Louis's IEP are structured boundaries including putting up his hand and not waving or shouting out in class. Given Louis's inclination for doing the minimum work required, he is not afforded opportunities for setting his own performance criteria such as those written in his IEP; these are set by teachers. Rewards, in the form of commendations and good letters from teachers, are written into Louis's IEP which is reviewed twice a year. His father is able to contribute to his IEP. Copies of all pupils' IEPs are contained in a book in the staffroom in order that teachers can access information about pupils.

The tendency for the LSA to focus her attention on Louis is beneficial at this stage in his schooling while he is still in the process of learning appropriate behaviour.

The LSA encourages Louis's inclusion with other children during groupwork activities in class. However, Louis often likes to be in control of groupwork, and this results in other pupils not wanting to work with him. According to the LSA, he either dominates groupwork or withdraws altogether and plays with his shoelaces. Louis sometimes undertakes groupwork activities with the LSA instead. The LSA feels it would be of more benefit if pupils engaged in groupwork with Louis.

There have been improvements in Louis's conduct in class. Like other children with autism he adhered to fixed routines previously, such as always sitting in the same seat in class. But as other pupils increasingly sat where he wanted to, his fixed routines abated. Progress made by Louis is in evidence in academic terms too, as commented on by his LSA: "He's pleased with himself this year because he's said, 'I've worked, I've managed to study and it's staying in'. He thought it was staying in his head more this year. So that was good.

The LSA is unequivocal in communicating her attitude to Louis. She praises him for good performance, but equally lets him know when, and why, he has not done well. She is reluctant to overly praise him for fear of misleading him. Praising Louis excessively may also engender a sense of complacency in him. Pupils with autism have individual problems that require support appropriate to their individual personalities. Based on their knowledge and experience of a pupil's personality, educators need to determine a balance of praise and constructive criticism in their endeavours to elicit the most favourable response from the child.

While there has been progress in some aspects of Louis's conduct, social interaction remains his most problematical area. He does not manage well in social situations, fluctuating between slipping into a dream world and being domineering. He says he has some friends, though his LSA is doubtful that he sees them socially out of school. According to the LSA, if other pupils are talking or not listening to him, he will raise his own voice to enter into a conversation: "He can hold the floor… But he's not really interacting with a group, he's just holding the group". The LSA pursues behaviour strategies with Louis, such as instructing him to listen and wait for an opportunity to talk rather than 'barging into a conversation'.

Louis has the additional problem of interpreting words literally. As a way of developing his understanding of language, the LSA is at times intentionally sarcastic to him, which he is able to recognise. In spite of these difficulties, one of Louis's passions is drama and acting and he very much enjoyed being involved in a play at school. Staff are seeking ways to extend Louis's involvement in drama, both within and outside school, in the belief that this may provide opportunities for him to develop the skills of communication, joining in and turn-taking.

The view of the SENCo

Staff are keen for Louis to have input on social behaviour outside the arena of mainstream classes. The SENCo identified social skills and life skills that Louis requires help with, such as crossing the road, asking for directions and asking for items in a shop. Although there is a recognised need to help Louis in these areas, the SENCo explained that the school does not currently have sufficient staffing resources. The SEN department is endeavouring to employ another full-time member of staff. If this is achieved they will withdraw Louis from mainstream class for two periods a week to focus on social skills. Planning Louis's withdrawal from mainstream lessons has involved the SENCo liaising with other agencies outside school. She is in consultation with an LEA educational psychologist and an educational psychologist from a local autistic support group to establish the nature of work to be undertaken with Louis when they withdraw him.

Another professional outside school with whom the SENCo liaises is a speech and language therapist who submits an annual report on Louis.

The SENCo discerned that pupils with Asperger syndrome can fall in between areas of provision. Professional agencies exist for dealing with mental health, educational psychology and speech and language therapy, yet children with Asperger syndrome do not come under any of these umbrella areas. For example, they may need speech and language therapy, but in its broadest sense in terms of facial expression, intonation and interpretation of meaning – akin to that required by Louis. Because children with Asperger syndrome do not fit neatly into any of these categories of provision, the SENCo highlighted the importance of support groups more tailored to their needs. Consultative groups focusing on children with autism and Asperger syndrome can indeed provide a forum for SEN staff and class teachers to share information and strategies for supporting pupils (Connor, 1999, p. 85). SEN staff at the case-study school benefit from a consultative group of this kind. They attend a support group held every other month, where different strategies are discussed and talks are given by guest speakers.

Conclusion

Each of the case studies described children with autism in different learning environments, and showed how the schools have adapted to meet the individual needs of the child. Provision was found within a primary classroom, a specialist base within a secondary school, a support facility for pupils with language disorders and a secondary school, all with varying levels of support and resources. Whilst staff had an opportunity to discuss the advantages and disadvantages they perceived within the provision, it is true to say that each school had clear benefits for educating the children in the ways that they did. As highlighted at the beginning of this book, these children were able to learn within the curriculum framework but they all displayed significant problems with the social aspect of learning; for example how they managed in the context of the classroom and their social peer relationships.

Clearly the notion of social inclusion is one that many schools have to address. How this is achieved is dependent upon schools acknowledging the need for diversity, not just in terms of the school population but also within the curriculum and pastoral support that it offers. A social model of inclusion has to take into account a more flexible approach towards the curriculum and the changes that can be made to the way subjects are taught (Robertson, 1998). The introduction of Citizenship within the National Curriculum will certainly pave the way for educating pupils about disability and diversity.

The adaptations that had been made to support the pupils in the case studies showed that whilst there were variations in the ways in which the children accessed the curriculum, they had all shown significant progress in terms of developing greater independence and autonomy over their own learning. Again in the changing climate of education, this is a phenomenon which is gradually encompassing schools. It may well have come about as a result of including more children with special needs into mainstream schools.

These different models of inclusive practice are a reflection of the current ways in which teaching professionals are addressing the special educational needs of children. The debate as to whether children with autism should be included or segregated is one which is no different from teaching others pupils who have a disability. It does demand that an understanding of the nature of the learning difficulties, a clear assessment of the resources required to maintain an adequate education, adaptations to the learning environment, and flexibility in the delivery of the curriculum need to be acknowledged by schools and Government inspectors alike. For the individual, and also for the parents of a child with autism, the school has to help them feel that they are part of the school community, and that there is a positive commitment on the part of staff to ensure that learning is an enjoyable experience. Once this is established it invariably follows that the rest of the pupils are more accepting of another child's 'way of being', and social relationships grow out of this positive ethos.

References

Armstrong F (1995), *Language Through the Curriculum, Equality of Access*, cited in Potts P, Armstrong F, Marsterton M (eds), *Learning, Teaching and Managing in Schools*, Routledge.

Attwood T (1998), *Asperger's Syndrome, A Guide for Parents and Professionals*, Jessica Kingsley.

Barnes J (1996), *Pupils With Asperger Syndrome: Classroom Management*, Essex County Council Education Department.

Carpenter B, Ashdown R, Bovair K (eds) (1996), *Enabling Access, Effective Teaching and Learning for Pupils with Learning Difficulties*, David Fulton.

Connor M (1999), 'Children on the autistic spectrum: Guidelines for mainstream practice', *Support for Learning, British Journal of Learning Support*, Vol. 14, No. 2, pp. 80-86.

Cumine V, Leach J, Stevenson G (1998), *Asperger Syndrome, A Practical Guide for Teachers*, David Fulton.

DfEE (1994), *Code of Practice on the Identification and Assessment of Special Needs*.

DfEE (1998), *Special Educational Needs Action Programme*.

DfEE (1998), *Supporting the Target Setting Process*.

DfEE (1999) *The National Curriculum*.

DfEE (2000), *Revised Draft Code of Practice*.

Grandin T (1996), *Thinking in Pictures: And Other Reports from My Life With Autism*, Vintage.

Jordan R, Powell S (1995), *Understanding and Teaching Children with Autism*, Wiley and Sons.

Jordan R (1996), *Strategies for the Education of Individuals with Autism*, Paper presented to The Sussex Autistic Society, University of Sussex, 9th November.

Jordan R, Powell S (1997), *Autism and Learning – A Guide to Good Practice*, David Fulton.

Jordan R, Jones G (1999), *Meeting the Needs of Children with Autistic Spectrum Disorders*, David Fulton.

Peacock G, Forrest A, Mills R (1996), *Autism: The Invisible Children*, National Autistic Society.

Preston M, 'Including Children with Autistic Spectrum Disorders', *Special Children* (Nov. 1998).

Robertson C (1998), 'The social model of disability and the rough ground of inclusive education' in *Enabling Inclusion: Blue Skies...Dark Clouds?*, T O'Brien (ed), London: The Stationery Office.

Seach D (1998), *Autistic Spectrum Disorder, Positive Approaches to Teaching Children with ASD*, NASEN.

Stainback S, and W (1992), *Curriculum Considerations in Inclusive Classrooms*, Paul H. Brookes Publishing Co.

West Sussex County Council (1996), *Autism and Asperger Syndrome*.

Williams D (1996), *Autism, An Inside-Out Approach*, Jessica Kingsley.

Wing L (1996), *The Autistic Spectrum – A guide for parents and professionals*, Constable.

Special CHILDREN

Supporting Children Series

The *Supporting Children* books are aimed at educational practitioners, both teachers and learning assistants, in specialist and non-specialist settings. Each book provides theory to inform the reader about a specific special need, while the main body of the text offers practical advice, support and activities to facilitate pupils' learning.

Supporting Children with Dyslexia

Supporting Children with Dyslexia focuses on the practical difficulties facing dyslexic pupils every day in every classroom. It presents a large number of ideas to enable teachers and parents to support dyslexic children and enable them to be included in the classroom. It encourages class teachers to reflect on their teaching and to develop their skill in meeting the needs of a wide range of pupils.

Price: £17.50   **ISBN:** 1-84190-085-0   **Format:** A4 Approx. 105pp

Supporting Children with ADHD

This book, with an introduction for teachers, is a photocopiable resource for children with ADHD. The activities and advice aim to enable these children to control their own feelings, thoughts and actions. By utilising the information provided, pupils with this complex personality type will realise they have a gift and not a disorder.

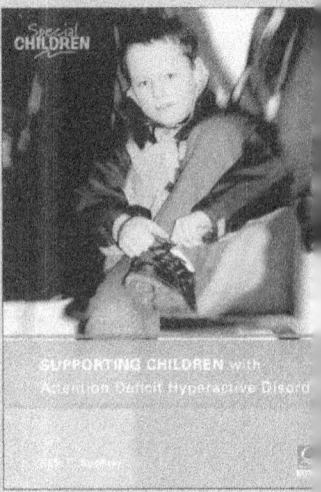

Price: £15.00   **ISBN:** 1-84190-056-7   **Format:** A4 Approx. 88

Supporting Children with Multiple Disabilities

By following the practical framework provided, teachers will be able to implement a multi-sensory curriculum in the classroom. This will enable children with multiple disabilities to become more independent and active, and to develop effective communication skills.

Price: £20.00   **ISBN:** 1-84190-042-7   **Format:** A4 Approx. 18(

Supporting Children with Speech and Language Impairment and Associated Difficulties

How do you identify pupils with speech and language impairment? This guide outlines the main areas of difficulty for pupils, and suggests how teachers can make the curriculum more accessible and so facilitate greater learning.

Price: £17.50   **ISBN:** 1-84190-083-4   **Format:** A4 Approx. 12